**SCHOLASTIC**

W9-AXH-894

# Professor Grammar's
# Punctuation Packets

Fun, Reproducible Learning Packets That Help Kids
Master All the Rules of Punctuation—Independently!

Capitalization Exclamation Points
Quotation Marks
Question Marks
Periods Colons
Commas
Apostrophes
And More!

by **Marvin Terban**
as *Professor Grammar*

New York • Toronto • London • Auckland • Sydney
Mexico City • New Delhi • Hong Kong • Buenos Aires

**Teaching** *Resources*

*To my wonderful granddaughter, Summer:*
*You punctuate my life with exclamation points!*

Scholastic Inc. grants teachers permission to photocopy the reproducible pages in this book for classroom use. No other part of this publication may be reproduced in whole or in part, or stored in a retrieval system, or transmitted in any form or by any means, electronic, photocopying, recording, or otherwise, without written permission of the publisher. For information regarding permission, write to Scholastic Inc., 557 Broadway, New York, NY 10012-3999.

Development Editor: Liza Charlesworth
Edited by Eileen Judge
Cover design by Maria Lilja
Cover illustration by Elliot Cowan
Interior design by Holly Grundon
Interior illustrations by Maxie Chambliss (pp. 13, 25, 27, 48, 50); Steve Cox (p. 37); Jason Robinson (p. 35)

ISBN: 978-0-545-20459-0

Copyright © 2011 by Marvin Terban, Scholastic Teaching Resources
Illustrations © 2011 by Scholastic Inc.
Published by Scholastic Inc.
All rights reserved.
Printed in the U.S.A.

5  6  7  8  9  10        40        18  17  16  15  14  13

# Contents

Introduction: *Who Says Punctuation Can't Be Fun?* . . . . . 4

How to Use This Book . . . . . . . . . . . . . . . . . . . . . . . . . . 5

Meeting the Standards. . . . . . . . . . . . . . . . . . . . . . . . . . 6

## Punctuation Packets

Commas I . . . . . . . . . . . . . . . . . . . . . . . . . . . . . . . . . . . . 7

Commas II . . . . . . . . . . . . . . . . . . . . . . . . . . . . . . . . . . . 15

Capital Letters I . . . . . . . . . . . . . . . . . . . . . . . . . . . . . . 23

Capital Letters II . . . . . . . . . . . . . . . . . . . . . . . . . . . . . 31

End Punctuation:
      Periods, Question Marks, Exclamation Points . . . . 39

Apostrophes . . . . . . . . . . . . . . . . . . . . . . . . . . . . . . . . . 47

Quotation Marks . . . . . . . . . . . . . . . . . . . . . . . . . . . . . . 55

Colons and Semicolons . . . . . . . . . . . . . . . . . . . . . . . . 63

Answer Key . . . . . . . . . . . . . . . . . . . . . . . . . . . . . . . . . 71

# Who Says Punctuation Can't Be Fun?

Hello! I'm Marvin Terban, also known as Professor Grammar. I know that some people think grammar is boring. Not me. I think it's exciting and fun. Without it, I'd be lost. And my goal with this book is to make grammar fun for you to teach and for kids to learn.

Some of your students will ask: *Why do we need to know about grammar when everyone already understands what we're saying?* When kids ask me that question, I reply: *How can a carpenter build a bookcase if he doesn't know what a hammer, a saw, or nails are?* If we don't know the right way to build a bookcase, we might manage to put something together, but it probably won't be very sturdy or functional. Similarly, *how can a writer build a sentence if she doesn't know what verbs, nouns, or adjectives are?* Knowing about grammar is important for effective communication.

In fact, there are many aspects of grammar that are critically important, and I show students how much we depend on them. Capital letters, for instance, help us tell the difference between a *lima* bean and *Lima*, Peru, and let us know we're buying furniture *polish* and not *Polish* ham. (I'd hate to polish my favorite table with a ham!)

But punctuation is my favorite part of grammar. I love punctuation! Punctuation marks are more than just little dots, curves, and squiggles. They're like road signs. A comma tells us to pause, while a period says, "Stop." (In Great Britain, a period is actually called a "full stop.") Semicolons are the perfect in-between punctuation marks because they're stronger than commas but weaker than periods. Knowing about apostrophes tells us when it's right to write *it's* or *its*.

I've always loved grammar, ever since I was in elementary school. After college, I began teaching grammar, which was the best job in the world for me. I tried to come up with fun ways for my students to learn grammar, and soon they started calling me Professor Grammar. Then teachers and parents started calling me Professor Grammar, too, and the name stuck.

Because I love punctuation so much, I've written this book all about punctuation. The material features some of the examples and activities I use in my own classroom. I've tried to make the worksheets interesting, challenging, and enjoyable. They're really more like word games than worksheets. Who says punctuation can't be fun? Not Professor Grammar! And with these activities neither will your students!

*Professor Grammar's Punctuation Packets* fits in perfectly with my other Scholastic books—on idioms (*Dictionary of Idioms*), spelling (*Dictionary of Spelling*), grammar (*Checking Your Grammar*), research skills (*Ready! Set! Research!*), and vocabulary (*Building Your Vocabulary*).

So get ready to have some fun teaching about punctuation. Those marks are little, but they're powerful, and they love to have fun. You can't even tell a "Knock, Knock" joke without using plenty of punctuation. Here's one to help make learning about punctuation lots of fun.

**Knock, knock.**

**Who's there?**

**Norma Lee.**

**Norma Lee who?**

**Normally, people think punctuation is boring, but in this book, it's fun!**

I hope you and your students will end up loving punctuation as much as I do!

— *Professor Grammar*

# How to Use This Book

The eight packets in this book target specific punctuation skills, including correct use of commas, capital letters, periods, question marks, exclamation points, apostrophes, quotations mark, colons, and semicolons. Each packets is a self-contained series of fun and engaging practice activities for a specific punctuation skill or set of skills that go together. Each skill is introduced, defined, and made clear with examples. Students then practice that skill by doing the activities. Each packet culminates with a fun, Tic-Tac-Toe style skill review that allows students to test their mastery of the punctuation skill they've been practicing. In general, the activities progress from simple applications of the skill to more difficult ones, and most of the solutions make the activities self-checking as well. However, an answer key is provided at the back of the book. The first page of each packet features a convenient checklist of the activities, so students can keep track of those they have completed.

**Assemble the packets:** Make two-sided photocopies of each packet. Be sure that the pages are in order, with the example and checklist sheet on top, then staple together.

## Here are suggestions for making best use of the punctuation packets:

**Reinforce your language arts curriculum:** These packets are a perfect way to practice punctuation skills that are part of your current language arts curriculum. If your curriculum includes instruction in grammar and punctuation, these packets are a great way to reinforce what you've taught. For example, if you've been working on commas, you might give students the commas packet as homework, independent work, or center work.

**Assess mastery of targeted punctuation skills:** You can also use the packets as a way to help students review skills they've been learning, then use the sheets to assess whether the entire class or individual students need additional practice.

**Introduce the packets as needed:** Even if your language arts curriculum does not include specific grammar and punctuation studies, your students will certainly benefit from practice with punctuation skills. Every teacher has read student work and realized that a certain student, or even the entire class, could use a lesson on capitalization, apostrophes, or quotation marks. When that happens, introduce and discuss the skill to be reviewed, then make copies of the appropriate packet for the whole class or for those students who need practice. Students can do the packets at home or at designated times in your class schedule.

**Keep it simple:** Whether your curriculum plan includes punctuation or your students just need some extra review, these punctuation packets offer simple, engaging, and fun ways to give students the practice they need without taking time away from your scheduled lesson plans. The straightforward format and the clear presentation of content make them perfect for independent work or homework.

# Meeting the Standards

The activities in this book are designed to help support you in meeting national and state language arts standards.

## Connections to the McREL Language Arts Standards

Mid-continent Research for Education and Learning (McREL), a nationally recognized nonprofit organization, has compiled and evaluated national and state standards—and proposed what teachers should provide students in grades 3–6 to grow proficient in language arts. This book's activities support the following standards:

Uses conventions of spelling in written compositions:

spells high frequency, commonly misspelled words from appropriate grade-level list; uses a dictionary and other resources to spell words; uses initial consonant substitution to spell related words; uses vowel combinations for correct spelling; uses contractions, compounds, roots, suffixes, prefixes, and syllable constructions to spell words

Uses conventions of capitalization in written compositions:

titles of people; proper nouns (names of towns, cities, counties, and states; days of the week; months of the year; names of streets; names of countries; holidays); first word of direct quotations; heading, salutation, and closing of a letter

Uses conventions of punctuation in written compositions:

uses periods after imperative sentences and in initials, abbreviations, and titles before names; uses commas in dates and addresses and after greetings and closings in a letter; uses apostrophes in contractions and possessive nouns; uses quotation marks around titles and with a comma for direct quotations; uses a colon between hour and minutes; use commas for tag questions, direct address, and to set off words

Uses appropriate format in written compositions:

uses italics (for titles of books, magazines, plays, movies)

Source: Kendall, J. S., & Marzano, R. J. (2004). *Content knowledge: A compendium of standards and benchmarks for K-12 education.* Aurora, CO: Mid-continent Research for Education and Learning. Online database: http://www.mcrel.org/standards-benchmarks/

## Common Core State Standards

The activities in this book also correlate with the English Language Arts standards recommended by the Common Core State Standards Initiative, a state-led effort to establish a single set of clear educational standards whose aim is to provide students with a high-quality education. To learn more, go to: www.corestandards.org

*Professor Grammar's Punctuation Packets* • © 2011 by Marvin Terban • Scholastic Teaching Resources

# Commas I

Commas are like little road signs that say "pause for a second." They group words together or separate them from the rest of the words to make sentences easier to read. Without commas, we'd have a very hard time figuring out a sentence like this:

> Yes Julius Caesar salad is on the menu along with chicken fingers frogs' legs and dessert.

Now let's put in all the missing commas and see how much easier it is to read:

> Yes, Julius, Caesar salad is on the menu, along with chicken fingers, frogs' legs, and dessert.

## Commas help us by

- ✔ separating words in a list or series
- ✔ setting off a mild interjection from the rest of the sentence
- ✔ separating clauses at beginnings of sentences
- ✔ preventing confusion when certain words are together
- ✔ setting off the greeting and closing of a letter
- ✔ showing who's being spoken to

In this packet, you'll learn several uses of the comma by doing fun activities and word games.

## Check off each activity page after you finish it.

- ☐ I. Commas: in a list or series
- ☐ 2. Commas: with interjections
- ☐ 3. Commas: after introductory clauses and phrases
- ☐ 4. Commas: between words that might cause confusion
- ☐ 5. Commas: in the greeting and close of a letter
- ☐ 6. Commas: in direct address
- ☐ Commas Tic-Tac-Toe

# 1

# Commas

## Activity Directions

In the sentences below, put in the missing commas where they belong. Then circle the letter that comes right after each comma you have inserted. The letters you circled will spell out the answers to the animal questions.

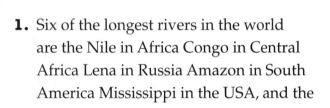

## Punctuation Rule

Use commas to separate three or more words and phrases (groups of words) in a series to make it easier for people to read your sentences. Example: *I put lettuce, tomatoes, cucumbers, and cheese in my salad.*

Notice that there is a comma before the words *and cheese* in the example above. This is called a "serial comma." Although not all writers use it, the comma before *and* and the last item in a series is what most people prefer. You should use it, too, to be right up to date with your punctuation.

1. Six of the longest rivers in the world are the Nile in Africa Congo in Central Africa Lena in Russia Amazon in South America Mississippi in the USA, and the Yangtze in China.

   What's a kind of shellfish?
   Answer:_____

2. Earth Jupiter Uranus Mars Pluto (a dwarf planet) Saturn, and Neptune are some of the planets in our solar system.

   What does a kangaroo do?
   Answer: He _____

3. William Shakespeare wrote many great plays like *Hamlet King Lear Othello As You Like It Love's Labours Lost* and *Macbeth.*

   What is a small Australian animal that lives in eucalyptus trees?
   Answer: _____

4. Goslings squabs hatchlings ephynas eyases polliwogs, and fawns are the names of baby geese, pigeons, dinosaurs, jellyfish, hawks, frogs, and deer.

   What's a woolly farm animal?
   Answer: _____

5. Some of the instruments in an orchestra are violins horns oboes organs flutes saxophones, and drums.

   What are the hard coverings over the feet of horses?
   Answer: _____

6. My favorite animated movies are *Up Ratatouille Alice in Wonderland Bambi Beauty and the Beast Ice Age Toy Story Shrek,* and *Happy Feet.*

   What are bunnies?
   Answer: _____

*Professor Grammar's Punctuation Packets* • © 2011 by Marvin Terban • Scholastic Teaching Resources

# 2

# Commas

## Punctuation Rule

Put a comma after a mild interjection (like *oh, yes, aha, well,* and *uh-huh*) at the beginning of a sentence.

**Note:** An interjection is a word or short phrase that expresses a feeling like surprise, pleasure, disgust, or amazement. It usually comes at the beginning of a sentence.

## Activity Directions

Put commas where they belong after the mild interjections in the sentences below. (Careful! Not all the sentences have interjections.) Then circle the first letter of the word that comes right after the comma. The letters you circled will spell out the answer to the riddle at the end.

1. My brother really doesn't like peanut butter and mushroom sandwiches.

2. My goodness rabbits can hop fast when they want to.

3. Gosh all my licorice melted in the sun.

4. Yuck cotton candy really sticks to your face, doesn't it?

5. My dear friend from camp is visiting this weekend.

6. Uh-oh everybody just went out the wrong door.

7. Oops Carl squirted ketchup on my new shirt.

8. Oh dear a page from my homework just blew out the window.

9. Gee whiz raccoons broke into the kitchen and ate Grandma's apple pie.

**Riddle**    What very fast vehicle is spelled the same backwards and forwards? (Hint: The answer can be spelled as one or two words.)

Answer: ___ ___ ___ ___ ___    or    ___ ___ ___ ___ ___    ___ ___ ___

# 3
# Commas

## Activity Directions

In the e-mail below, put in all the missing commas where they belong after clauses and phrases at the beginnings of sentences.

### Punctuation Rule

**Put a comma after a clause or phrase (including a prepositional phrase) at the beginning of a sentence.** This kind of clause usually begins with a word like *before, after, although, because, in, on, over, under, unless, whether,* etc.

---

From: Summerv22@happycamp.org
To: Bestgrandma@kryt.com
Subject: My first week at camp

Dear Grandma,

Although I've been here for only one week I've already made a lot of new friends. Because kids come here from my school I knew some of them already. Since this camp is right on a lake we do a lot of water sports like swimming and boating. Unless it's really raining we're outside all day long. After the swim across the lake we had a picnic. Before the talent show yesterday I had to practice singing with my mouth full of pretzels. I won for funniest act! If you can come on visiting day that would be awesome. Until I see you again stay well.

Hug Fluffy for me.

Love,

Summer

Note: The e-mail addresses above are not real.

*Professor Grammar's Punctuation Packets* • © 2011 by Marvin Terban • Scholastic Teaching Resources

# 4

# Commas

## Punctuation Rule

**Use commas between certain words that might cause confusion together.** The comma will separate the words, making readers pause slightly to think about what they are reading. For example:

This sentence—without the comma— is confusing.

*If he calls his mother will know where he is.*

With the comma, the sentence is very clear.

*If he calls, his mother will know where he is.*

## Activity Directions

The sentences below don't make sense because some commas are missing. Please put commas between some of the words to make sure the sentences are not confusing. Add just one comma to each sentence. Circle the letter after each comma you put in. The circled letters will spell out the answer to the riddle at the end.

1. When the mosquitoes came out in went the people.

2. While they were flying nine planes flew in front of them.

3. Outside the bedroom carpet the hallway.

4. Though we believe in recycling our brother doesn't.

5. After you read the book report on it to the class.

6. Please tell Paul Revere is a city in Massachusetts.

7. When he began painting everyone said he needed art lessons.

8. To make ice chill water.

9. Before they finished eating the chicken flew away.

10. To Abraham Lincoln seemed like a good capital for Nebraska.

11. Inside your grandpa's barn was noisy.

## Riddle

Which word is spelled incorrectly in every dictionary?

Answer: ___ ___ ___ ___ ___ ___ ___ ___ ___ ___ ___

# 5

# Commas

**Punctuation Rule**

Use commas after the greeting (salutation) and closing of a friendly letter. Greetings usually begin with *Dear*, and closings are words like *Love, Cordially, Sincerely, Very truly yours*, etc.

## Activity Directions

What if you and your friends could actually write to any of the presidents of the United States, living or dead. Several such letters are below, but they're not complete. Some commas are missing! The presidents won't like that. So make sure to add in all the commas after the greetings and closings.

Dear President Washington

Is it true that you had wooden teeth? If so, what did you brush them with, sandpaper?

Sincerely yours

Renae Young

**Dear President Grant**

**I heard you once got a speeding ticket for riding your horse too fast in Washington, DC. Who paid the fine, you or the horse?**

**Yours truly**

**Rachel Jenn**

Dear President Garfield

I read that you could write in Latin with one hand and in Greek with the other hand—at the same time! Could you write any languages with your feet?

Your friend

Valentine Sums

Dear President Jefferson

Some people say you invented the coat hanger, the fold-up bed, the dumbwaiter, the swivel chair, a letter-copying machine, the lazy Susan, and the pedometer. When did you have time to write the Declaration of Independence and be president?

Respectfully

Annabell Callie

Dear President Obama

It says in your biography that when you played basketball in high school in Hawaii, you had such a great jump shot that people called you O'Bomber. Are you sorry you never became a professional basketball player instead of president?

Be well

Gabriel Hayden

**Dear President Lincoln**

**Is it true that an 11-year-old girl first suggested that you grow a beard? I think more presidents should take advice from kids.**

**Best wishes**

**Edward David**

# 6

# Commas

## Punctuation Rule

Use one or two commas to set off a noun of direct address at the beginning, middle, or end of a sentence. The "noun of direct address" is the word or words that name the person who is being spoken to directly.

Examples:

*Ladies and gentlemen, the show is about to begin.*

*Thanks, Dad, for helping me with my homework.*

*Your new cat really meows loudly, Sue.*

## Activity Directions

Here are some riddles. Put commas where they belong to set off the nouns of direct address.

 What is full of holes Amanda but stills holds water?

A sponge Justin.

 Which weighs more Steve a pound of feathers or a pound of iron?

Jane they both weigh a pound.

 Why didn't the skeleton go to the dance Sophie?

Because Matt he had no body to go with.

 Dennis why did Dracula's mother get him cough medicine?

Because of his coffin Lynda.

# Punctuation
# Tic-Tac-Toe COMMAS I

Which of the sentences below have all the commas where they should be? Mark each correct sentence by putting an X in the little checkbox. Get three Xs in a row and you win! Tic-Tac-Toe can be vertical, horizontal, or diagonal. Hint: There are two ways of winning the game below.

| | | |
|---|---|---|
| **1** My favorite authors are J. K. Rowling, Dr. Seuss, Maurice Sendak, and Judy Blume. | **2** Gosh I never knew our teacher could sing opera like that. | **3** When the stage lights came on, on came the jugglers. |
| **4** You can't bring an alligator to school Roslyn even if he is your best friend! | **5** Hello, everyone, and welcome to the zoo. | **6** Dear Harriet, Come visit me in Vermont. Love, Len |
| **7** I told George Washington is both a city and a state. | **8** Pitch the tent gather logs open the sleeping bags and then we'll camp out. | **9** Since it's raining so hard, we'll have to postpone the pig races. |

Fix the sentences that are not punctuated correctly by putting in the commas where they belong.

 *Professor Grammar's Punctuation Packets* • © 2011 by Marvin Terban • Scholastic Teaching Resources

**Check off each activity page after you finish it.**

☐ I. Commas: multiple adjectives

☐ 2. Commas: main (independent) clauses

☐ 3. Commas: appositives

☐ 4. Commas: non-essential phrases and clauses

☐ 5. Commas: dates and addresses

☐ 6. Commas: quotations

☐ Commas Tic-Tac-Toe

Name:_____

Date Due: _____

# Commas II

A comma is like a traffic officer for sentences. It tells you when to slow down, pause, or go ahead and move around something—like switching lanes. Commas do this by organizing the words in a sentence. They help make sentences easier to read by keeping words together in groups (like clauses and quotations), preventing a pile-up by separating words (like adjectives and appositives), and signaling any information that isn't absolutely necessary.

Without commas, some sentences would be very tricky to understand, like this one:

> Ash Jen's big fat fluffy cat who was born in Jersey City New Jersey sleeps late eats a lot and screeches "Meeee-ooooow!" if you step on her tail.

Now let's put in all the missing commas and see how much easier it is to read.

> Ash, Jen's big, fat, fluffy cat, who was born in Jersey City, New Jersey, sleeps late, eats a lot, and screeches, "Meeee-ooooow!" if you step on her tail.

## Commas help us by

✔ separating multiple adjectives for the same noun
✔ grouping clauses together
✔ separating nouns from their appositives
✔ setting off words that are not important to the meaning of the sentence
✔ punctuating dates and addresses correctly
✔ setting off quotations (people's exact words) from the rest of the sentence

In this packet, you'll learn several uses of commas by doing fun activities and word games.

# 1

# Commas

## Activity Directions

Below is a flyer from a big shopping mall. The products on sale are described with lots of appealing adjectives, but the commas that are supposed to separate them are missing. Please add them so that the flyer can be given out to customers.

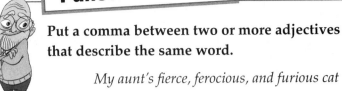

**Punctuation Rule**

Put a comma between two or more adjectives that describe the same word.

*My aunt's fierce, ferocious, and furious cat licked my face.*

If the word "and" could go between two adjectives, that's where the comma would go.

*My uncle's sweet and gentle dog bit me!*
*My uncle's sweet, gentle dog bit me!*

("sweet and gentle"= "sweet, gentle")

## Marvelous Mall Shopping Guide
### TODAY'S SPECIALS

| | | | |
|---|---|---|---|
| *Lorraine's Luscious Lemons & Limes*<br><br>FRESH JUICY FRUITS<br>*right off the tree* | **Shana's Shoes**<br><br>**Stylish Chic Affordable Footwear for Those Special Nights Out** | Ed & Esther's Electronics<br><br>The latest greatest most amazing new gadgets in stock! | *Karen's Kids' Clothing*<br><br>DARLING ADORABLE DELIGHTFUL FASHIONS FOR YOUR CHILDREN |
| **Barbara's Bed & Bath**<br><br>**Puffy Fluffy Towels and Smooth Soft Sheets** | Tiger's Terrific Toys<br><br>LOVABLE HUGGABLE BEARS TO BE YOUR BEST FRIENDS | *Jen's Jewels*<br><br>GORGEOUS SPARKLING ELEGANT RINGS AND BRACELETS | **FREEDMAN'S FURNITURE**<br><br>**Comfortable durable sofas to make your home more livable** |
| **Lorrie's Lovely Lollipops**<br><br>**flavorful juicy treats on sticks** | Roslyn's Restaurant<br><br>TASTY SCRUMPTIOUS DELECTABLE DISHES TO PLEASE YOUR TASTE BUDS | Lexi's Linens<br><br>Elegant Exclusive Luxurious Bedspreads and Comforters for a Great Night's Sleep! | **HARRIET'S HATS**<br><br>Fabulous Fashionable Feathered Chapeaus for Those Special Occasions |

# 2

# Commas

## Activity Directions

In the Sentence-Making Machine below, three short sentences go in one side, and one longer sentence comes out the other. Help the machine do its work by adding commas where they belong between main clauses.

## Punctuation Rule

**Put commas between main clauses (also called independent clauses) in a sentence when there are at least three clauses.** A main or independent clause is a group of words that could stand alone as a sentence.

For example: *My mom plays the flute. My dad dances. My brother sings.*

You can combine these short sentences into one much more interesting sentence by using commas, like this: *My mom plays the flute, my dad dances, and my brother sings.* (What a musical family!)

## The Sentence-Making Machine

| | |
|---|---|
| It rained on Monday. It snowed on Tuesday. It was nice on Wednesday. | It rained on Monday snowed on Tuesday but was nice on Wednesday. |
| Gerry has a cat. Lynette has a dog. I have a canary. | Gerry has a cat Lynette has a dog and I have a canary. |
| The hamburger was delicious. The hot dog was tasty. The dessert was great. | The hamburger was delicious the hot dog was tasty and the dessert was great. |
| Justin could ride his bike to school. He could take the bus. He could walk. | Justin could ride his bike to school he could take the bus or he could walk. |
| The horse neighed loudly. The kitten purred softly. The pig didn't say a thing. | The horse neighed loudly the kitten purred softly but the pig didn't say a thing. |
| At the party, Margo recited a poem. Mike played the guitar. Max told jokes. | At the party, Margo recited a poem Mike played the guitar and Max told jokes. |

# 3

# Commas

## Activity Directions

Below is a mini-book of fun facts about famous folks. All the commas that are supposed to separate the appositives from the nouns they refer to are missing. Please add them, so the sentences will be easier to read.

## Punctuation Rule

**Use one or two commas to separate a noun from its appositive.** Appositives are words that give information about the noun they follow. In the sample sentences below, the words in italics (*slanty letters*) are appositives. Without the commas, these sentences would be difficult to read.

My grandfather, *the mayor of Prattville*, has a curly beard.

My grandfather, *the man with the curly beard*, is the mayor of Prattville.

The man with the curly beard is my grandfather, *the mayor of Prattville*.

The mayor of Prattville is the man with the curly beard, *my grandfather*.

# Fun Facts About Famous Folks

| | | |
|---|---|---|
| Marion Moon was the mother of Buzz Aldrin the second man on the moon. | Vincent van Gogh the famous painter sold only one painting in his whole life – to his brother! | Marie Curie the first woman to win a Nobel Prize won it twice! |
| Bill Gates the computer genius wrote his first computer program at thirteen. | Samuel Langhorn Clemens was the real name of Mark Twain the author of *Tom Sawyer*. | General George Custer the youngest man ever to become a general in the U.S. Army graduated last in his class at West Point. |
| Sally Ride the first American woman to ride into space answered a newspaper ad looking for people who wanted to be astronauts. | Shirley Chisholm an African-American Congresswoman from New York ran for president in 1972. | John Quincy Adams president of the U.S. from 1825 to 1829 kept a pet alligator in the White House. |
| Isabella Baumfree was the birth name of Sojourner Truth the American abolitionist in the 1800s. | Charles Dickens the author of *Oliver Twist* slept facing north because he thought it improved his writing. | Sandra Day O'Connor the first woman on the Supreme Court has a school named after her in Phoenix, Arizona. |

*Professor Grammar's Punctuation Packets* • © 2011 by Marvin Terban • Scholastic Teaching Resources

# 4

# Commas

## Activity Directions

Below is another Sentence-Making Machine. A full sentence goes in one side, along with extra words and phrases that are not really needed. A sentence with those nonessential words comes out the other side. Put commas around the words that are not essential to the meaning of the sentence.

### Punctuation Rule

Put a comma before and after words in a sentence that are not essential—that are not really important to the meaning of the sentence.

If you leave non-essential words out, the sentence still makes sense. For example:

*Professor Wilson, who has an adorable son named Reinhart, always begins his Latin classes by saying, "Salvete."*

The words between the commas are not essential (important) to the main meaning of the sentence. They may add interest, but the sentence would be fine without them.

*Professor Wilson always begins his Latin classes by saying, "Salvete."*

## The Sentence-Making Machine

| | |
|---|---|
| These shoes don't match that dress. which are a size 8 | These shoes which are a size 8 don't match that dress. |
| A giraffe cleans its ears with its tongue. which can stand as tall as 18 feet | A giraffe which can stand as tall as 18 feet cleans it ears with its tongue. |
| Balloons and cactus plants don't mix. as you can see | Balloons and cactus plants as you can see don't mix. |
| My grandfather loves to climb trees. who is almost 90 years old | My grandfather who is almost 90 years old loves to climb trees |
| Eat plenty of fruits to be healthy. especially oranges | Eat plenty of fruits especially oranges to be healthy. |
| Ms. Jannetta is my history teacher. not Ms. Allen | Ms. Jannetta not Ms. Allen is my history teacher. |
| The Eiffel Tower is in Paris, France. which opened in 1889 | The Eiffel Tower which opened in 1889 is in Paris, France. |
| The music is way too loud. in my opinion | The music in my opinion is way too loud. |

# 5

# Commas

**Punctuation Rule**

Put commas in dates and addresses in sentences, like this:

Between the date number and the year: *January 20, 2009*

After the year: *On January 20, 2009, the Obamas moved in to the White House.*

Between the street address and the city: *1600 Pennsylvania Avenue, Washington, DC*

Between the city and the state (or district): *Washington, DC*

After the whole address: *1600 Pennsylvania Avenue, Washington, DC, is where the White House is located.*

Here's where all those commas go in one sentence:

*On January 20, 2009, Barack Obama and his family moved into 1600 Pennsylvania Avenue, Washington, DC, after he became President of the United States.*

## Activity Directions

Below are instructions to the people who work for a pet store delivery company. It would make their jobs much easier if there were commas where they belonged in the instructions below. Please put in all the missing commas according to the rule at right.

# PET EXPRESS
## We Deliver Everything, From Ants to Elephants

This porpoise goes to 51 Grove Street Jade MN on June 20 2013 and don't drip water on the carpet when you carry it inside.

Mrs. Laurie at 6 Stoney Brook Lane Glenn ND needs this rhinoceros no later than June 22 2013 and don't stick yourself on its horn.

Rush this giraffe to 6 Ledgewood Way Bonnie NE before February 14 2013 and be careful going under bridges and overpasses.

The anteater must arrive at 39 Stanwood Road Scottswamp OH on November 7 2011 and take this jar of ants along for snacks

On December 4 2012 carry this hippo to 1610 Lenox Ave. Dylan FL and you'd better take a few extra men with you.

Make sure this shipment of alligators gets to 99 Avenue B Summy IL by July 22 2012 and don't stick your fingers into the cage.

Dispatch these butterflies to 66 Madison Avenue Edward MS by August 28 2012 and never open the carton to look in.

Transport this bald eagle to 5 Greenbriar Road Howard TX by December 19 2011 and don't muss its hair.

This peacock goes to 2100 Shumard Oak Lane Irving MA by November 5 2011 and be careful of its feathers.

Send this kangaroo to 12 Cottonwood Avenue Judi NY no later than March 12 2012 and don't let it jump around too much.

## 6

# Commas

### Activity Directions

A reporter for a school newspaper was assigned to ask teachers what their favorite things were. Her article is printed below, but it's missing the commas that go with the direct quotations. Please add them in.

### Punctuation Rules

**Use commas to set off direct quotations.** A direct quotation (or quote) is the exact words someone says.

**When you quote someone, put a comma after a word that means anything like** *said* (*shouted, whispered, answered, cried, moaned,* etc.) **and before the first set of quotation marks,** like this: Jennifer said, "My daughter's name is Summer."

**Put a comma before, or inside, the second set of quotation marks 1) if the direct quote is a statement (not a question or exclamation), and 2) if the sentence continues after the quote,** like this: Jennifer said, "*My daughter's name is Summer,*" and then she smiled.

Note: If the quote is an exclamation or question, put an exclamation point or question mark inside the second set of quotation marks, like this: "*Can you babysit Summer on Wednesday?*" *asked Jennifer.* [No comma before *asked* here because the quote gets a question mark.]

# What's Your Favorite Thing?

### by Wendy Words

I asked Ms. Konokowski, the math teacher, what her favorite food was. She answered "Chocolate-covered worms, of course."

Mrs. Scotto, another math teacher, said her favorite people were her grandsons. "Matt and David" she stated "are cuter than worms."

Mrs. Millan, the lady in the corner office, loves the environment. "*Clean Up the World* is the best TV show" she declared.

Mr. Greenblatt, the substitute teacher, stated "My favorite animal is Madison, my cat, because she sleeps with me each night."

Ms. Soares, the language teacher, said "My favorite movie is *Vampires Eat New Jersey.* I watch it all the time."

When I asked Ms Cho, the school nurse, what her favorite color was, she answered "Chartreuse" and then she added "with a slight touch of magenta."

# Punctuation
# Tic-Tac-Toe  [COMMAS II]

Which of the sentences below have all the commas where they should be? Mark each correct sentence by putting an X in the little checkbox. Get three Xs in a row and you win! Tic-Tac-Toe can be vertical, horizontal, or diagonal.

| | | |
|---|---|---|
| **1** The giant cucumber which I found on the subway grows in only one place in the world: a tiny island near Hawaii. ☐ | **2** My darling granddaughter was born on June 22  2007 in New York  NY. ☐ | **3** Take this money jump on your bike ride to the store and get me a dozen worms so that we can go fishing. ☐ |
| **4** Mike shouted to Linda from the train window "Don't forget the knishes!" ☐ | **5** Aaron is a big tall handsome smart young man with a great sense of humor. ☐ | **6** This *cornutia grandifolia* flower which I got from a friend in Florida attracts butterflies and hummingbirds. ☐ |
| **7** She picked up the bat, walked up to the plate, swung fiercely at the ball, and hit a home run out of the park! ☐ | **8** Peach melba and melba toast, two foods I love, were named after Nellie Melba, a famous opera singer. ☐ | **9** Arlene whispered, "I think I left Jack's porcupine on the school bus." ☐ |

Just for FUN!

Fix the sentences that are not punctuated correctly by putting in the commas where they belong.

 *Professor Grammar's Punctuation Packets* • © 2011 by Marvin Terban • Scholastic Teaching Resources

## Check off each activity page after you finish it.

- [ ] I. Capital Letters: the first word in a sentence or quotation

- [ ] 2. Capital Letters: proper nouns and adjectives

- [ ] 3. Capital Letters: days, months, holidays, events

- [ ] 4. Capital Letters: brand name products, companies, etc.

- [ ] 5. Capital Letters: in titles

- [ ] 6. Capital Letters: Mixed Practice

- [ ] Capital Letters Tic-Tac-Toe

# Capital Letters I

Capital letters have pretty big functions. They start the names of specific people, places, and things (proper nouns), and begin days of the week, months, holidays, and special events. They identify brand names and are used for the main words in the titles of books, movies, songs, and the titles of courses at school. Since they are bigger than a period (which ends a sentence), they make it easier to see when a new sentence is beginning!

Without capital letters, reading sentences and paragraphs would be very difficult. For example:

> over memorial day weekend in may, we went to boston to visit my brother david at chelsea university. he took me to bag of books and bought me a copy of *a palace of pickles*. then we went to sue's snacks for lunch. he told me, "you'll like it," and I really did.

Now let's put in all the missing capital letters and see how much easier it is to read.

> Over Memorial Day weekend in May, we went to Boston to visit my brother David at Chelsea University. He took me to Bag of Books and bought me a copy of *A Palace of Pickles*. Then we went to Sue's Snacks for lunch. He told me, "You'll like it," and I really did.

## Capital letters highlight

- ✔ when sentences and direct quotations begin
- ✔ nouns that name specific persons, places, and things
- ✔ days, months, holidays, and special events
- ✔ brand names of products
- ✔ main words in titles of books, movies, plays, etc.

In this packet, you'll learn several uses of capital letters by doing fun activities and word games.

# 1

# Capital Letters

**Punctuation Rule**

Capitalize the first word in a sentence or in a direct quotation. A direct quotation is the exact words a person says.

## Activity Directions

In each sentence below, circle two letters that should be capitalized according to the punctuation rule above. Next, read the question that follows the sentence. Print the two letters that you circled on the two blank lines of the "Answer." A third letter is already there. If you capitalized correctly, all three letters create the answer to the question. (Note: The answers are the initials of well-known expressions, organizations, or things, like *LOL* and *USA*.)

1. talking very softly, she said, "love your porcupine, but don't hug it ."
   What should you always treat babies with?
   Answer: _____ _____ C

2. don't ever say, "vampire bats are cute," in my house!
   What do you call a shiny disk with a movie on it?

   Answer: _____ _____ D

3. very often my aunt would shout, "ice is cold!"
   Who is a celebrity, star, or a prominent public figure?

   Answer: _____ _____ P

4. recently they announced, "igloos don't make good homes in the desert."
   What is written on many tombstones?

   Answer: _____ _____ P

5. inside the mountain, the caveman was singing, "rocks really rock!"
   Who collects taxes for the government?

   Answer: _____ _____ S

6. uncle George mumbled, "feathers tickle," and then he sneezed.
   What is an unidentified object in the sky called?

   Answer: _____ _____ O

7. now I'm going to tell her, "flamingos don't belong in the kitchen."
   What is an organization of football teams?

   Answer: _____ _____ L

8. fortunately Grandma whispered, "bananas are sometimes green."
   What US government organization investigates crimes?

   Answer: _____ _____ I

# 2

# Capital Letters

## Activity Directions

Circle all the letters that should be capitalized in the sentences below. The letters you circle will spell out the answers to the animal question for each sentence.

**Punctuation Rule**

Capitalize proper nouns and proper adjectives, including languages. A proper noun is a word that names a specific person, place, or thing. *Jennifer*, *Japan*, and *Jello* name a specific woman, a country, and a brand-name dessert and should be capitalized. A proper adjective comes from a proper noun; *American*, *Chinese*, and *Shakespearean* are proper adjectives.

1. My cousin, georgio ingelbert from russia, met his girlfriend, alberta feather, in france on top of the eiffel Tower.
   What tall mammal can clean its ears with its tongue?

   _____

2. On my tour, I went to edinburgh and london (where they speak english), then to paris, havana, amsterdam (in the netherlands), and tokyo.
   What mammal can drink up to 80 gallons of water a day, live to be at least 70 years old, purr like a cat, but can't jump?

   _____

3. albert long moved from long island to georgia, and then to abilene, texas, where he ate popcorn made by orville redenbacker.
   What animal cannot move backwards?

   _____

4. In hamburg, iowa, penelope pepper sent an e-mail to her friend in orlando.
   What animal gives birth under water?

   _____

5. max oblong, from netawaka, kentucky, married his girlfriend edith while jumping out of a plane over yonkers.
   What animal uses tools more than any other animal except for humans?

   _____

6. The swiss man who drank turkish coffee swam the amazon river, while his friend fred walked from ireland to sweden speaking hindi!
   What fish doesn't have a brain?

   _____

7. My cousins went to three colleges: miami university, loyola, and emerson.
   What animal has a horse for a mother and a donkey for a father?

   _____

8. In hungary, the names of actual cities are ibrany, nagyatad, and nagykanizsa, but not ypsilanti, which is in another place entirely.
   What animal has a donkey for a mother and a horse for a father?

   _____

# 3

# Capital Letters

## Punctuation Rule

Capitalize the days of the week, months of the year, holidays (religious and non-religious), festivals, and special events. Do not capitalize the seasons (summer, fall/autumn, winter, spring) unless they are part of the name of a special event, like "Florida Fall Festival."

## Activity Directions

Something must have gone wrong at the company that printed a new calendar because a lot of the capital letters were left out. Below are some pages from that calendar. Circle the thirteen letters that should be capitalized. Write them on the dotted lines at the bottom. The letters will spell out the name of the most heartfelt holiday of the year.

| | | | |
|---|---|---|---|
| Wednesday, November 11 <br><br> **veterans Day** | Monday, January 26 <br><br> **asian Lunar New Year** | Monday, September 7 <br><br> **labor Day** | Saturday–Monday, September 19–21 <br><br> **eid-al-Fitr** |
| Thursday, December 31 <br><br> **new Year's Eve** | tuesday, July 4 <br><br> **independence Day** | Tuesday, november 3 <br><br> **election Day** | sunday, April 4 <br><br> **Easter** |
| Friday, June 22 <br><br> **dog and Cat Appreciation Day** | Friday, April 23 <br><br> **arbor Day** | Monday, September 28 <br><br> **yom Kippur** | |

**Riddle**

The letters that should be capitalized spell out a heartfelt holiday:

Answer:

___ ___ ___ ___ ___ ___ ___ ___ ___ ,  ___ ___ ___ ___

**4**

# Capital Letters

**Punctuation Rule**

Capitalize brand name products and the names of companies and stores.

## Activity Directions

Below, circle the letters that should be capitalized. Each letter you circle begins the name of a popular brand, company, store, and so on. Those letters will spell out names of baseball teams. Write the team names on the lines. See if you can hit a home run and name each team!

1. tylenol bat wheaties ball  iams shoe nike spalding nut

   Baseball team:

   _____

2. foot  benetton rayovac fish alpo ant vaseline exxon tree subaru

   Baseball team:

   _____

3. hat macy's book ebay spoon toyota scissors lamp sunkist

   Baseball team:

   _____

4. alka seltzer phone lane  tums tie rolex olympus  radio scholastic

   Baseball team:

   _____

5. candle crayola bubble uniroyal door buick stroller baby starkist

   Baseball team:

   _____

6. brush rubbermaid button energizer horse dell bus samsung park

   Baseball team:

   _____

7. geico light ihop taxi amazon.com fence nintendo foot texaco sears

   Baseball team:

   _____

8. ear pampers bird adidas car duracell toe reebok epson banana starburst

   Baseball team:

   _____

9. maytag applebee's seat raisinettes dog lipton izod eye nabisco snickers

   Baseball team:

   _____

10. texas instruments bag fruit general electric taxi radio shack

    Baseball team:

    _____

# Capital Letters

**5**

## Activity Directions

In the posters below, circle all the letters that should be capitalized in the titles of books, plays, etc. The letters you circle will spell out the names of birds.

### Punctuation Rule

Capitalize the first word, the last word, and all the main words in titles of books, movies, albums, songs, plays, musicals, magazines, newspapers, video games, and television shows. Capitalize all nouns, pronouns, and verbs. Don't capitalize small words like conjunctions (*and, or, but*, etc.), articles (*the, a, an*), or prepositions (*to, for, in, of, by*, etc.) unless they're the first or last words in the title or have at least four letters.

Note: Titles are usually put into *italics* (or underlined if handwritten), except for the titles of songs, stories, and poems, which are put in quotation marks.

**1.** BEST-SELLING BOOK!

*how to amuse the whiskers of a kitten*

Bird: _____

**2.** HIT SONG!

"give us lots of love"

Bird: _____

**3.** BLOCKBUSTER HORROR FILM!

*terror everywhere! right now!*

Bird:

_____

**4.** AWARD-WINNING ANIMAL TV SHOW!

*octopuses, walruses, and lizards*

Bird: _____

**5.** SOLD-OUT BROADWAY PLAY!

"let's all raid the kitchen"

Bird: _____

**6.** CHART-TOPPING ALBUM!

*dragons and unicorns can't kiss*

Bird: _____

**7.** EXERCISE MAGAZINE!

*judo, acrobatics, and yoga*

Bird: _____

**8.** GREAT BROADWAY MUSICAL!

"castle of raindrops, ocean of wonder"

Bird: _____

**9.** POPULAR NEWSPAPER!

*kentucky independent world inquirer*

Bird: _____

**10.** WORLD'S BEST VIDEO GAME!

*weird reptiles and eerie nests*

Bird: _____

*Professor Grammar's Punctuation Packets* • © 2011 by Marvin Terban • Scholastic Teaching Resources

**6**

# Capital Letters I: Mixed Practice

**Practice Makes Perfect!**

On this page, you can practice all the rules about capital letters that you've learned in this packet.

## Activity Directions

In the sentences below, some of the letters that should be capitalized are not—the first words of sentences or direct quotations; the beginning of proper nouns and proper adjectives; days of the week, months, holidays, and special events; brand names and names of companies or stores; and main words in the titles of books, movies, songs, TV shows, video games, and so on.

**World Capitals?** Circle the letters that should be capitalized. Write those letters on the blank lines below. The letters will spell out the name of a country.

**1.** Last night on *hopping around the Globe,* I watched "Inside india" and "touring iceland."

\_\_\_\_  \_\_\_\_  \_\_\_\_  \_\_\_\_  \_\_\_\_

**2.** I'm reading two great books: *pickles everlasting* and *A rainy Day in uruguay.*

\_\_\_\_  \_\_\_\_  \_\_\_\_  \_\_\_\_

**3.** karen said, "elephants don't live in new york (except in zoos), aaron."

\_\_\_\_  \_\_\_\_  \_\_\_\_  \_\_\_\_  \_\_\_\_

**4.** On my world tour, I ate cheerios in uganda and Raisin bran in albania.

\_\_\_\_  \_\_\_\_  \_\_\_\_  \_\_\_\_

**5.** jennifer shouted to alexandra, "please stop andrew from eating nana's cookies!"

\_\_\_\_  \_\_\_\_  \_\_\_\_  \_\_\_\_  \_\_\_\_

**6.** In New York City, you can see the empire State Building, visit grant's Tomb, go to a game at yankee Stadium, picnic in Central park, and gaze at the lights in times Square all in one day!

\_\_\_\_  \_\_\_\_  \_\_\_\_  \_\_\_\_  \_\_\_\_

**7.** columbus Day and halloween are in the fall, independence Day and labor Day are in the summer, and easter is in the spring.

\_\_\_\_  \_\_\_\_  \_\_\_\_  \_\_\_\_  \_\_\_\_

**8.** We stayed at the tumbledown inn and ate at burrito eat-O! on tuesday.

\_\_\_\_  \_\_\_\_  \_\_\_\_  \_\_\_\_  \_\_\_\_

# Punctuation
# Tic-Tac-Toe  Capital Letters I

Which of the nine sentences below have all the capital letters where they should be? Mark each correct sentence by putting an X in the little checkbox. Get three Xs in a row and you win! Tic-Tac-Toe can be vertical, horizontal, or diagonal. Hint: There are two ways of winning the game below.

| | | |
|---|---|---|
| **1** If you ever meet my cousin, never ask her, "Do you like radishes?" | **2** Jennifer loves Japanese food, but David eats only Danish dishes. | **3** I saw a display of Cuisinart coffee makers at Macy's. |
| **4** Amazingly, the book *My little Turtle* was made into the play *Petunias for Penelope*, then into the movie *thunder on miami*. | **5** Six presidents of the United States were named James: Madison, Monroe, Polk, Buchanan, Garfield, and Carter. | **6** On my trip, to europe, I ate french food in France and Swiss cheese in switzerland. |
| **7** There are four or five sundays in every march. | **8** I wrote a letter to the TV station when my favorite show, *Monkeys From mars*, was taken off the air. | **9** The class jumped for joy when the teacher announced, "There will be no homework tonight!" |

Just for FUN!

Fix the sentences that are not punctuated correctly by putting in the capital letters where they belong.

 *Professor Grammar's Punctuation Packets* • © 2011 by Marvin Terban • Scholastic Teaching Resources

**Check off each activity page after you finish it.**

☐ I. Capital Letters: regions vs. directions

☐ 2. Capital Letters: historical events and documents

☐ 3. Capital Letters: greetings and closings of letters

☐ 4. Capital Letters: a person's official title

☐ 5. Capital Letters: titles of family members

☐ 6. Capital Letters: Mixed Practice

☐ Capital Letters Tic-Tac-Toe

Name: _____

Date Due: _____

# Capital Letters II

If you know when to use capital letters, you can identify historical events and show respect for people and their titles, such as *President Washington* and *Mrs. Norden*. You can show the difference between a direction (*Go north two blocks*) and a region (*I live in the North*). You can write the greetings and closings of letters, and even know when to write *Uncle* or *uncle*.

Without capital letters, things get confusing:

> dear aunt olive
>
> Yesterday grandma told me that during world war II, grandpa Samuel and uncle George lived in the northwest but traveled east and served in the army under general Battleman.
>
> yours truly,
>
> Maya

See how it looks when we use capital letters:

> Dear Aunt Olive,
>
> Yesterday Grandma told me that during World War II, Grandpa Samuel and Uncle George lived in the Northwest but traveled east and served in the army under General Battleman.
>
> Yours truly,
>
> Maya

## Capital letters help us identify

- ✔ the difference between regions of a country and directions
- ✔ historical events and documents
- ✔ greetings and closings in letters
- ✔ official titles and titles of family members

In this packet, you'll learn several uses of capital letters by doing fun activities and word games.

# 1

# Capital Letters

## Activity Directions

Below are some postcards that people have sent from their travels. Circle eight words that need to be capitalized because they name regions of the USA.

## Punctuation Rule

**Capitalize North, South, East, West, Northeast, Northwest, Southeast, Southwest, and Midwest when they refer to specific regions.** For example: *She was born in the West but lived in the East when she went to college.*

*Note:* Do not capitalize north, south, east, or west when they refer only to directions, like this: *Drive west for ten miles and then turn north at the waterfall.*

**Here's a tip:** In the example, notice that the word "the" comes before the region word. This usually means you should capitalize it: *She was born in the West but lived in the East when she went to college.*

**Here's another tip:** If the direction word ends in *–ern*, it usually does not need a capital letter: *The hurricane hit the eastern seaboard pretty hard.*

---

Hello, Grandma,

We're in the south enjoying Florida, but we miss our relatives in the north, so we'll soon be driving north to see you. Miss ya!

   Renae

---

Dear Uncle Johnny,

We're flying west towards Nevada over the Rocky Mountains.  Those things are tall!

   See you soon,
   Isla

---

Dear Georgia cousins,

It's pretty cold in the northwest today. I'll bet you're all nice and toasty in the southeast. Brrrrr!

   Your cousin from Oregon

---

What's up, guys?

We're camping out near the Grand Canyon in the southwest. That thing is deep!

   Valentine

---

Salutations, Mom and Dad,

I'm traveling east from the midwest, so in a few days, I'll be back east and can visit you in Philadelphia.  I'm having fun.  Send money!

   Your son, Dave

---

Dear Terri,

I'm visiting my grandparents in the great northeast this summer.  Tomorrow we're driving south from Boston to Washington, DC. I'll say "Hi!" to the president for you.

   Pete

---

*Professor Grammar's Punctuation Packets* • © 2011 by Marvin Terban • Scholastic Teaching Resources

# 2

# Capital Letters

## Punctuation Rule

Capitalize historical events, periods, and documents, like these:

*Korean War, Louisiana Purchase Treaty, the Ice Age*

## Activity Directions

Below is a listing of programs on the History-Mystery TV channel. Circle all 34 letters that should be capitalized according to the rule above.

| THE HISTORY-MYSTERY CHANNEL | | |
|---|---|---|
| Where the Past Is Our Present to You! | | |
| **MONDAY** | | |
| 8:00 to 9:00 p.m. | 9:00 to 10:00 p.m. | 10:00 to 11:00 p.m. |
| **medieval Times:** What were the middle ages in the middle of? | **The First Ten Amendments:** Was the bill of rights right? | **Men in Armor:** How hot and heavy were those trojan war suits? |
| **TUESDAY** | | |
| 8:00 to 9:00 p.m. | 9:00 to 10:00 p.m. | 10:00 to 11:00 p.m. |
| **When People Are Revolting:** The french revolution vs. the american revolution | **The Great Charter:** What the magna carta really says about King John | **Quill Pen:** How Jefferson wrote the declaration of independence without a computer |
| **WEDNESDAY** | | |
| 8:00 to 9:00 p.m. | 9:00 to 10:00 p.m. | 10:00 to 11:00 p.m. |
| **Freeing the Slaves:** We unlock the emancipation proclamation. | **North vs. South:** What was civil about the civil war? | **Know-It-Alls:** Were people smarter during the renaissance just because they knew everything? |
| **THURSDAY** | | |
| 8:00 to 9:00 p.m. | 9:00 to 10:00 p.m. | 10:00 to 11:00 p.m. |
| **Brother, Can You Spare a Dime?:** Why the great depression wasn't so great! | **Mighty Metals:** Was the bronze age better than the iron age? | **The Long, Long War:** Why the crusades lasted 200 years! |
| **FRIDAY** | | |
| 8:00 to 9:00 p.m. | 9:00 to 10:00 p.m. | 10:00 to 11:00 p.m. |
| **You're Right!:** What the united states constitution means to you | **Breaking Up Is So Hard:** The reasons for the war of independence | **The gettysburg address:** It isn't 1600 Pennsylvania Avenue. |

**3**

# Capital Letters

## Punctuation Rule

**Capitalize the first word in the greeting and the closing of a friendly letter,** like this:
*Dear Ms. Kilmer; Hey there; Hello; everyone; Warm regards; Your friend; Many thanks; Lots of love*

## Activity Directions

Here are some important letters that are stuck in the post office. They can't be delivered without capital letters in the greetings and closings. Please circle the 12 letters that should be capitalized according to the rule above.

*To Joan of Arc:*

my dear Miss Arc,

I really admire you because you were shorter than I am and you still led an army.

    rock on,
    Justin

*To Ben Franklin*

good morning, Mr. Franklin,

Did you know what was going to happen when the lightning hit the key or were you shocked?

    sincerely,
    Jessica and Aaron

*To Thomas Edison:*

hello, Mr. Edison,

Thanks for inventing the light bulb.  I can read much better at night now.

    brightly yours,
    Amanda

*To William Shakespeare:*

hark, Will,

When my brother forgot our apartment number, he asked, "2B or not 2B?"  I guess he got that from you.

    cheerio,
    Shana

*To the Wright Brothers:*

greetings, Orville and Wilbur,

How come your first flight lasted only 120 feet?  You could have just walked that far, right?

    over and out,
    Jade Leong

*To Isaac Newton:*

kind Sir,

Is the Fig Newton named after you?

    yours truly,
    Sasha

**4**

# Capital Letters

## Activity Directions

Below is the Hall of Statues of Famous People. The signs under the statues are missing some capital letters. Circle the nine letters that should be capitalized according to the rule at right.

## Punctuation Rule

**Capitalize official titles in front of people's names.** For example: *At the meeting, Vice-President Paul Chapman gave a great speech.*

(Don't forget to capitalize the names after the titles. They're proper nouns.)

*Note:* Do not capitalize the title if it is used without the person's name, like this:

*At the meeting, the vice-president made a great speech.*

president
Millard McKinley

governor
Alphonse Mutter

mayor
Horatio Hopper

senator
Gilbert Moose

king Albert III

lord
Reginald Mountbatty

duchess
Frederica Fishy

prime minister
Wallace Waffle

# 5

# Capital Letters

## Activity Directions

Below are some notes that people left on refrigerators. Circle the eleven letters that should be capitalized according to the rule at right.

## Refrigerator Notes

**Punctuation Rule**

Capitalize the titles of family members ("relative" words) when you are using that title as the person's name. Relative titles are words like mom, dad, mother, father, aunt, and uncle.

*Here are three hints about when to use a capital letter:*

1. **When you refer to specific family members without their names or use a relative word as a person's name:** *Tell Mom that Dad is home. I love Grandma.* (Note: Do not use a capital letter in this sentence: *I love my grandma.* In this case "grandma" is not being used as the person's name. The same here: *My aunt is a doctor.*)

2. **When you speak directly to a family member,** like this: *I need money, Mom.*

3. **When family titles come in front of names,** like this: *Aunt Doris, Cousin Joanie.*

Party List: aunt Shirley, grandpa Lester, and cousin Sybil.

Tell dad the dog buried the remote control in the backyard.

Jed,

Please get mom some worms for her pet bird when you go to the market. Don't forget!

Did grandma give grandpa a motorcycle for his birthday? Cool!

Is aunt Olive bringing the hot dogs or the buns?

At 9 a.m., granny is going to be interviewed on the *Hello, Everyone!* show.

Find out if my grandfather made relish.

Remember to give nana Rachel her umbrella with the bamboo handle.

## 6

# Capital Letters II: Mixed Practice

**Practice Makes Perfect!**

Here's your chance to practice the rules about capital letters you learned in this packet.

### Activity Directions

Below are some notes found in bottles **floating** in the ocean. They were written so fast that there wasn't time to put in all the capital letters. Now you have plenty of time. Circle all the letters that should be capitalized in the notes below.

I was sailing west to find the east, but I bumped into a new world.

best wishes,

captain C. Columbus

---

dear anyone,

**Help!**

sincerely,

Lost at Sea

---

Inside this bottle is a copy of the bill of rights. Please pay the bill for it, okay?

---

I never liked the duke of wellington at the battle of waterloo.

Defeatedly,

emperor Napoleon

---

Hi, mom and dad,

I'm sailing northeast then southwest around the world. I won't be home for dinner.

love,

Richard

# Punctuation
# Tic-Tac-Toe | Capital Letters II

Which of the nine sentences below have all the capital letters where they should be? Mark each correct sentence by putting an X in the little checkbox. Get three Xs in a row and you win! Tic-Tac-Toe can be vertical, horizontal, or diagonal. Hint: There are two ways of winning the game below.

| | | |
|---|---|---|
| **1** If you live in the southwest, you'd better have a good air conditioner. ☐ | **2** Every Easter, I love to make colorful eggs and roll them on the lawn. ☐ | **3** If you drive north for three days, you'll come to the cities of the northeast. ☐ |
| **4** In mythology class, we read about Apollo, the god of the sun, medicine, archery, poetry, dance, music, and other stuff. ☐ | **5** My dear friend,<br><br>I hope you are well.<br><br>Best wishes,<br><br>Your secret admirer ☐ | **6** My favorite relative, Aunt Lorrie, always bakes the best chocolate chip cookies for Christmas. ☐ |
| **7** It was an honor to meet mayor Millan and governor Sanz yesterday. ☐ | **8** Dinosaurs roamed the Earth during the Triassic and Jurassic periods. ☐ | **9** Before they were married, mom and dad had dated in high school. ☐ |

Fix the sentences that are not punctuated correctly by putting in the capital letters where they belong.

*Professor Grammar's Punctuation Packets* • © 2011 by Marvin Terban • Scholastic Teaching Resources

Check off each activity page after you finish it.

☐ I. Question Marks

☐ 2. Exclamation Points: in exclamatory sentences

☐ 3. Exclamation Points: in forceful commands and strong interjections

☐ 4. Periods: after sentences that state facts

☐ 5. Periods: after mild imperative sentences

☐ 6. Periods: after abbreviations and initials

☐ End Punctuation Tic-Tac-Toe

Name:_____

Date Due: _____

# End Punctuation:
## Periods, Question Marks, Exclamation Points

Every sentence needs a punctuation mark at the end. We end sentences with periods, question marks, or exclamation points. Periods are also used in abbreviations and initials. Exclamation points are also used for interjections.

Here are some sentences without punctuation marks.

Look out for that falling boulder

Ouch  It hit my head  Why didn't you warn me sooner

Mr J J Rumpert is coming for dinner at 8 pm

Let's put in the missing punctuation and see how much better the sentences are.

Look out for that falling boulder!

Ouch! It hit my head! Why didn't you warn me sooner?

Mr. J. J. Rumpert is coming for dinner at 8 p.m.

## Periods help us by

✔ showing where a statement sentence ends

✔ showing where a mild command ends

✔ punctuating abbreviations and initials

## Question marks help us by

✔ identifying a question and showing where it ends

## Exclamation points help us by

✔ signaling strong interjections, commands, or emotions—and showing where these end

In this packet, you'll learn the uses of periods, question marks, and exclamation points by doing fun activities and word games.

# 1

# Question Marks

## Punctuation Rule

Use a question mark at the end of a question, like this:

Is your birthday on February 14 or July 19?

## Activity Directions

Below are several sentences without end punctuation marks. Seventeen are questions. Put question marks in the blank boxes at the ends of the questions. Then see what figure the question marks make.

What's your pet goat's name ☐   It snowed all week long, not just today ☐

Where is your house ☐   Is he your dog ☐   Once there were only ten months ☐

What is that ☐   Is this your red umbrella, sir ☐   The longest day is always in June ☐

Does anyone here know the way down to the field ☐   My grandma was the mayor ☐

Could you describe the bird that stole your big hat ☐   The snowman was 10 feet tall ☐

Grass is green ☐   Is the play going to start soon ☐   Camels have three eyelids ☐

Who was the first president on a postage stamp ☐   She tripped over a tree root ☐

If I lend you a dollar, will you pay it back soon ☐   October has thirty-one days ☐

Why did you say that to his favorite pet fish ☐   My cat had six kittens in May ☐

Mom, where was Grandfather born ☐   Mark Twain wrote Tom Sawyer ☐

Is this the stop for the art museum ☐   Your strongest muscle is your tongue ☐

Who is the man with the long coat ☐   A cheetah is the fastest animal on Earth ☐

Where did I hide my brother's hat ☐   Hawaii became the 50th state in 1959 ☐

Do you like my new blue sneakers ☐   The Hundred Years War lasted 116 years ☐

A jellyfish is mostly water ☐   Tuesday comes after Monday ☐   This is a frog ☐

Where will they go after that party ☐   Houdini's real name was Erich Weiss ☐

## 2

# Exclamation Points

## Activity Directions

Below are groups of three sentences. One sentence asks a question; one makes a statement; one expresses strong emotions. Put an exclamation point after the sentences that express strong emotions. (If you like, add the other end punctuation, too.) Then, circle the letters that come right before the exclamation points you added, and write them on the lines below. At the end, when you read the circled letters aloud; they will sound out the answer to the riddle.

**Punctuation Rule**

Use an exclamation point at the end of an exclamatory sentence (a sentence that expresses very strong feelings). Here are some sentences with powerful emotions:

*Joy:* It stopped raining so we can have the wedding outside!

*Fright:* There's a weird thing under my bed!

*Excitement:* We're winning! We're winning!

*Surprise:* John, you came to my party!

What is that loud sound
Run! it's an erupting volcano
That was just my stomach rumbling

A boa constrictor is crawling up my leg
It's a snake from Central and South America
How is that going to help me

Is there a police station around here
There's one next to the Italian pastry shop
Help, someone stole my cannoli

What act are you doing for the talent show
I'm dressing up as a duck and singing opera
That's amazingly fantastic

I will not dance in the ballet tonight
Why not, madam
I refuse to wear that totally terrible tutu

Here's the lion house at the zoo
How are you feeling, lion
Roar

Do you hear that loud buzzing
It's just a bumblebee
Ow! It just stung my arm

It's nice here in the woods
Did you hear that scary noise
It's Bigfoot

**Riddle**  What did the surprised bank robber say when he cracked open a safe with no money in it?

Answer: ___ ___ ___ ___ ___ ___ ___ ___ !

# 3

# Exclamation Points

**Punctuation Rule:**

Use an exclamation point after a strong interjection or at the end of a forceful command. An interjection is a word or group of words expressing emotions (usually at the beginning of a sentence). A command orders or insists that you do something.

After an interjection: *Oh, no! I just dropped my cell phone into the lake!*

After a command: *Stop that at once!*

Notice that a sentence that shows strong feelings ends with an exclamation point, too. It's called an exclamatory sentence.

## Activity Directions:
The four little poems that follow contain a lot of strong emotions. A total of 18 exclamation points need to be added. Please put them where they're needed after interjections and at the end of sentences.

When Asta the astronaut flew into space,
The sky was pitch black and not blue.
She shouted out, "Wow  What a wonderful place  "
And "Oh  What a marvelous view "

Hurray  Hurray  We won the prize
The golden cup is ours
The crowd yells, "Yeah  We love you guys "
And showers us with flowers.

Eek  A mouse is in my house
It ran across the floor
But I won't have to call my spouse,
'Cause phew  It just flew out the door.

When Little Lord Lonny came down with the flu,
The doctor came over and said, "Drink this goo."
Lonny screamed, "Ugh  That stuff tastes just like glue  "
And "Ouch  That big needle you gave me hurt, too "

# 4 Periods

## Activity Directions

Below are little conversations between people.
The sentences are missing their punctuation marks.
Some of the sentences are declarative (they make statements).
Others may ask a question or express strong emotions or commands.
Decide which sentences are declarative and state facts. Add periods
to the end of those sentences only.  Then, add up all the numbers
in front of the sentences that needed periods, and you'll have the
answer to the question at the end. (If you like, you can add question
marks and exclamation points to the other sentences.)

**Punctuation Rule**

Use a period at the end of
a declarative sentence (a
sentence that states a fact),
like this: *Hummingbirds can
fly backwards.*

1. The dinosaur is loose

2. What should we do

3. I am going to wave when it goes by

4. Is today Wednesday

5. It is

6. Yikes, I forgot to study for the math test

7. I like turpoljes

8. What are they

9. They're spotted pigs

10. I spotted one once

11. Why did you say that

12. What did I say

13. You said you like asparagus

14. I do

15. But why did you say it

16. Help  Help

17. What's the matter

18. An earthquake is shaking the house

19. That's just an elephant walking by

20. Money doesn't grow on trees

21. Then why do banks have branches

## Question

What number does the Roman numeral *C* stand for?

Answer: _____

# 5

# Periods

## Activity Directions

Below are sentences with no end punctuation. Put a period *only at the end of the sentences that are mild imperatives*, according to the rule at right. Circle the first letter of each imperative sentence, then put the letters in order on the lines below. They will spell out one of the longest words in English that has no repeated letters. It will also answer the question at the end. (Hint: It has 13 letters.)

## Punctuation Rule

**Use a period at the end of a mild imperative sentence.** A mild imperative gives a mild command, makes a request, or expresses a wish, like this:

Mild Command: *Sit in that seat.*

Request: *Pass the salt, please.*

Wish: *Have a happy birthday.*

A mild imperative sentence that begins with *will* can sometimes sound like a question: *Will you please shut the window.* This is really a request, not a question. For a simple request, put a period at the end of the sentence. If the sentence expresses strong emotion, put an exclamation point after it.

Sometimes imperative sentences tell a person what not to do, like this: *Don't speak.*

1. Take your purple umbrella today

2. Raise your hand if you know the answer

3. Yesterday was my canary's birthday

4. Why did you paint your eyebrows green

5. Open your books to the chapter on tap-dancing frogs

6. Did you get a text from Sue about the spider

7. Unbutton the baby's coat when you go inside

8. It rained on the parade, but we still had it

9. Before you eat, wash your hands

10. My niece's name is Jade, like the green stone

11. Let all the snakes out of their cages before you go home today

12. Enjoy yourself at the masquerade party

13. Move your baby dinosaur to the next cage

14. Ask questions if you don't understand something

15. The first president to go to the World Series was Woodrow Wilson, in 1915

16. Kiss your kangaroo to show you love it

17. Horses and cows sleep while standing up

18. Insert tab A into slot B

19. Never say "Ish-ka-bibble" to me again, please

20. Are you Mr. Greenblatt

21. Sharks lay the biggest eggs in the world

22. Get all your stuff and follow me

# Question

**What does a kid get sent to the principal's office for?**

Answer: ___  ___  ___  ___  ___  ___  ___  ___  ___  ___  ___  ___  ___

 *Professor Grammar's Punctuation Packets* • © 2011 by Marvin Terban • Scholastic Teaching Resources

# 6

# Periods

## Punctuation Rule

Use a period after abbreviations and initials, like this:

*Ms. Consuela K. Schlepkis was born at 8:14 a.m. on Aug. 14 in Washington, DC.*

## Activity 1 Directions

A conference of important people is about to begin. But the periods have been left out of the abbreviations on their name cards. Please put them in before the guests arrive. Then, write what you think each abbreviation stands for on the blank line.

## ABBREVIATIONS GAME

| | | |
|---|---|---|
| Hello, I'm<br>Gen Hickory Battle<br><br>_____ | Hello, I'm<br>Rep Reginald Law<br><br>_____ | Hello, I'm<br>Sen Phineas Filibuster<br><br>_____ |
| Hello, I'm<br>Rev Peter Pewter<br><br>_____ | Hello, I'm<br>Fred Feelgood, M D<br><br>_____ | Hello, I'm<br>Jacob Jabber, Jr<br><br>_____ |

## Activity 2 Directions:

Put the periods where they belong in these famous authors' initials. Then circle what you think the initials stand for.

## AUTHORS' INITIALS GAME

**J K Rowling**
(Harry Potter books)

1. Jane Karen

2. Joanne  Kathleen

3. Jillian Katherine

4. Josephine Kuthbert

**J R R TOLKIEN**
(*The Hobbit* and *The Lord of the Rings*)

1. John Ronald Reuel

2. Jacob Reese Randolph

3. Jerrold Robert Radcliff

4. Jeremiah Rufus Ransley

**C S Lewis**
(*The Chronicles of Narnia*)

1. Charles Stanford

2. Cecil Stevens

3. Clive Staples

4. Clyde Salisbury

# Punctuation
# Tic-Tac-Toe

Which of the sentences below have periods, question marks, and exclamation points in the right places? Mark each correct sentence by putting an X in the checkbox. Get three Xs in a row and you win! Tic-Tac-Toe can be vertical, horizontal, or diagonal. Hint: There are two ways to win the game below.

| | | |
|---|---|---|
| **1** It is always colder in winter than in summer. | **2** Flee. Run. Escape. A spaceship full of monsters has just landed in the schoolyard? | **3** In 44 BC, Julius Caesar was the boss of Rome! |
| **4** Don't eat that!  The cat licked it. | **5** Daddy, why is the grass green?  Why is the sky blue? | **6** If you mix blue and red together, you get purple? |
| **7** P. T. Barnum was a great circus owner in the late 1800s. | **8** Rats.  I just stepped in mud with my brand new shoes? | **9** Is the male peacock prettier than the female? |

Just for FUN!

Fix the sentences that are not punctuated correctly.

Name:_____

Date Due: _____

# Apostrophes

Apostrophes are handy for lots of things. They help nouns show ownership. (*Amy's* cat) They show where letters are missing in contractions. (*it's, you'll, don't*) They can even make numbers, lowercase letters, and symbols plural. (Dot your i*'s* and cross your t*'s.*)

In the example below, four apostrophes are missing from the sentence. Can you see where they go?

> Make sure theres no mistake on Blancas poster: "Hippopotamus" should be spelled with three ps and two os.

Here's where apostrophes should go:

> Make sure there's no mistake on Blanca's poster: "Hippopotamus" should be spelled with three p's and two o's.

## Apostrophes help us

- ✔ make singular and plural nouns show ownership
- ✔ make compound nouns show ownership
- ✔ show joint ownership and multiple possessives
- ✔ show where letters are missing in contractions
- ✔ make numbers, lowercase letters, and symbols plural

In this packet, you'll learn several uses of apostrophes by doing fun activities and word games.

**Check off each activity page after you finish it.**

- [ ] I. Apostrophes: singular possessives
- [ ] 2. Apostrophes: plural possessives
- [ ] 3. Apostrophes: compound possessives
- [ ] 4. Apostrophes: joint ownership and multiple possessives
- [ ] 5. Apostrophes: contractions
- [ ] 6. Apostrophes: plural numbers, letters, and symbols
- [ ] Apostrophes Tic-Tac-Toe

# Apostrophes

## Activity Directions

Every cubby below has something special in it that belongs to a child. Therefore, the names need to show ownership. You know how to do that. It's as easy as this: All singular possessive nouns end with 's. Make each name a possessive.

**Punctuation Rule**

To make a singular noun show ownership, just add 's—no matter what letters the word ends with.

Examples: *my boss's car, Justin's shoe, Luis's bat, Amanda's job, Mr. Burgess's dog*

| Aaron Cubby | Isla Cubby | Tiger Cubby |
|---|---|---|
| Olive Cubby | Roz Cubby | Carlos Cubby |
| Maya Cubby | Thomas Cubby | Judi Cubby |
| Cass Cubby | Jade Cubby | Charles Cubby |
| Ashley Cubby | Alexis Cubby | Brittany Cubby |

# 2
# Apostrophes

**Punctuation Rule**

Make a plural noun possessive (show ownership) by adding an apostrophe (') or apostrophe + s ('s), depending on the last letter of the word.

If the last letter of the plural noun is *s*, just add an apostrophe to make it possessive:

*actors' costumes, runners' sneakers, citizens' votes, clowns' tricks, babies' diapers*

If the last letter of the plural noun is <u>not *s*</u>, add *'s* to make it possessive, like this:

*deer's tracks, alumni's records, fish's tank*

## Activity Directions

Construction of the town's new Recreation Center is almost finished. Now the signs have to be put up. Oops! Someone has to fix the signs! Can you help? Look at the last letter of each of the plural nouns in bold type and decide if you should add an apostrophe (') or an apostrophe and an *s* ('s) to make the words possessive. Put the ' or *'s* where it belongs.

**BOYS   LOCKERS**

WOMEN   ROOM

EMPLOYEES ENTRANCE

LADIES CHANGING AREA

**GIRLS LOCKERS**

**MEN ROOM**

INSTRUCTORS LOUNGE

MICE   CHEESE STORAGE AREA

**PEOPLE   GARDEN**

**CHILDREN PLAYGROUND**

**3**

# Apostrophes

## Activity Directions

A big family is taking a trip together. Below is their packing list. Make sure to add *'s* wherever needed so that everything goes where it is supposed to.

**Punctuation Rule**

Add apostrophe + *s* (*'s*) to the end of singular compound nouns with hyphens to make them possessive (show ownership): *editor-in-chief's* desk.

A **compound noun** is made up of two or three words. Sometimes the words are combined into one word: *scare + crow = scarecrow*. Sometimes they stay as two separate words: *school bus*. Sometimes the words are connected by hyphens: *editor-in-chief*. When the compound noun is hyphenated, follow the rule above.

# PACKING LIST

1. sister-in-law  silver shoes in the red suitcase

2. great-grandmother  lace shawl in the large trunk

3. six-year-old  favorite books in the small trunk

4. brother-in-law  socks in the blue backpack

5. son-in-law  gym shorts in the green duffel bag

6. mother-in-law  wallet in the leather handbag

7. great-aunt  glasses in the over-the-shoulder bag

8. great-grandfather  suspenders in the valise

9. father-in-law  coonskin cap in the hat box

10. step-sister  fancy gown in the garment bag

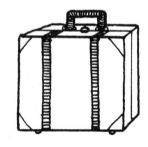

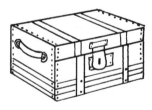

## Suitcase Joke

At a very noisy airport, a little boy proudly said to a lady, "I have a suitcase." She replied, "Yes, you do have a cute face."

# 4

# Apostrophes

## Activity Directions

These frames have no pictures. The words above the frames tell what the picture should be. Decide if the people in the pictures own an item together or if each person owns something separately. Then draw the picture. Add *'s* where it belongs in the caption under each picture.

## Punctuation Rules

To show joint ownership of one thing or to show possession of multiple things, here are rules to follow:

**When two or more people <u>own the same thing together</u>, put an apostrophe + s (*'s*) on the end of the final name:**

*Barbara and Howard's house* (Barbara and Howard own the same house together.)

*Jake, Josh, and Joe's hamster* (The three brothers own one hamster together.)

**When two or more people <u>own different things</u>, put an apostrophe + s (*'s*) on the end of each person's name:**

*Fatima's and Lourdes's houses* (Fatima and Lourdes have their own separate houses.)

*Aaron's, Jessica's, and Jade's toys* (Each child owns his or her own toys.)

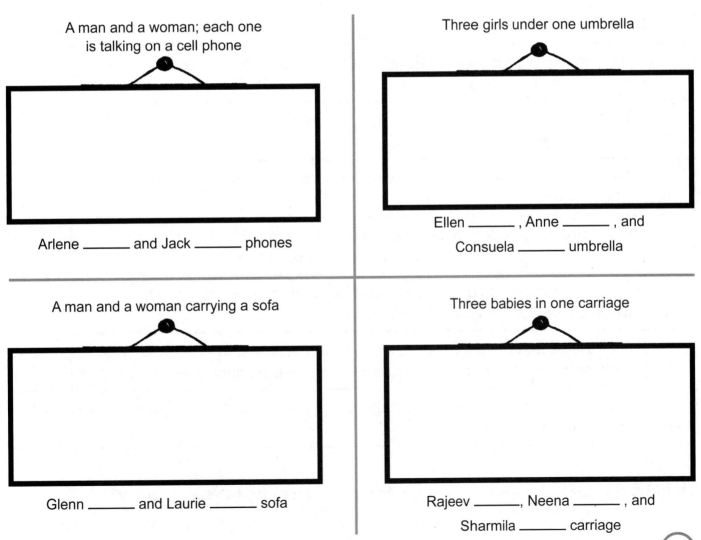

A man and a woman; each one is talking on a cell phone

Arlene _____ and Jack _____ phones

Three girls under one umbrella

Ellen _____ , Anne _____ , and Consuela _____ umbrella

A man and a woman carrying a sofa

Glenn _____ and Laurie _____ sofa

Three babies in one carriage

Rajeev _____ , Neena _____ , and Sharmila _____ carriage

# 5

# Apostrophes

**Punctuation Rule**

In contractions, put apostrophes where the missing letter or letters went. If you contract (squeeze) "is not" into one word and take out the letter *o*, it becomes "isn't." That's a contraction. The apostrophe goes where the *o* used to be. Sometimes more than one letter is missing: *They've = They have.*

## Activity Directions

In the sentences below, put apostrophes in the contractions where the letters have been omitted. Count the number of apostrophes you put in each sentence and write that number in the box provided. When you're finished, add up all the numbers. The correct sum will answer the math question at the bottom of the page.

| | | |
|---|---|---|
| 1. | She doesnt know if weve got enough money or if we havent. | |
| 2. | Shouldnt you be asking if well arrive on time or if wed be wise to turn back before its too late? | |
| 3. | Im sorry, but shell have to wait her turn or theyll all get angry before youve sung the song. | |
| 4. | My sister cant run that fast, so youll just have to slow down or shell make us go home earlier than wed expected. | |
| 5. | Theyre the ones hes been talking about because they wouldnt give him any cookies. | |
| 6. | Theyll love the new teacher because hes very nice, and thatll make them happy. | |
| 7. | Ive walked six miles to see them, but theyre not home, and they shouldve been, so thats all I have to say about that. | |
| 8. | Arent you worried that theres going to be a snowstorm tonight and we wont be able to go to school tomorrow? | |
| 9. | If he hadnt said what he said, she wouldnt have said what she said, and they wouldve had a better time at the party, dont you think? | |
| 10. | Whats that, and wheres the thingamajig, and whos he, and whens the show, and whod like to go? | |

## Question

How many arms are there on seven starfish and a monkey? _____

 *Professor Grammar's Punctuation Packets* • © 2011 by Marvin Terban • Scholastic Teaching Resources

# 6
# Apostrophes

## Activity Directions
These signs give good instructions, but some apostrophes are missing. Help fix the signs by putting in the apostrophes where they belong.

Tip: Some signs don't need any fixing.

> **MATH STUDENTS:**
> Don't confuse your 6s and your 9s.

> **TEST TAKERS:**
> Put ✓s in the boxes next to the correct answers.

> **GAME PLAYERS:**
> To play Tic-Tac-Toe, first draw a lot of # s.

> Handwriters:
> Carefully dot your i s and cross your t s .

> **High School Juniors:**
> Get DVDs to help you study for your SATs.

> **SPELLERS:**
> Be sure to spell "Mississippi" with four i s and "muumuu" with four u s .

> E-MAILERS:
> Put @s into all e-mail addresses.

> **EVERYBODY:**
> "Mind your p s and q s."
> (Behave yourselves.)

## Punctuation Rules

**To make lowercase letters plural, add 's,** like this:

*There are two a's at the beginning of "aardvark."* (Without the apostrophe, the *a's* would look like the word *as*, and that would be confusing.)

**To make symbols and punctuation marks plural, add 's,** like this:

*You painted the signs wrong. The ←'s should be →'s, so everybody's getting lost!*

*Don't put so many !'s at the end of your sentences. It makes you sound hyper.*

*Here's when NOT to use an apostrophe!*
**To make numbers, decades, and centuries plural, just add s:**
*There are two 3s in my phone number. Some great songs were written in the 1990s.*

***To make capital letters plural, just add s:**

*Little kids must learns their ABCs. Make sure your Es don't look like Fs.*

**Note:** The old rule to make numbers and capital letters plural was to add ('s), so you may come across this when reading: *Make sure your E's don't look like F's.* That's fine, but be sure to follow the new rule in your own writing: **just add s.**

# Punctuation
# Tic-Tac-Toe

Which sentences have all the apostrophes where they should be? Mark each correct sentence by putting an X in the checkbox. Get three Xs in a row and you win! Tic-Tac-Toe can be vertical, horizontal, or diagonal. Hint: There are two ways to win the game.

| | | |
|---|---|---|
| **1** The childrens' room is very messy. | **2** Ive always thought that it is'nt nice to say, "Wow that was loud!" when someone sneezes. | **3** In the 1800s, women wore big dresses. |
| **4** The mens room is on the fourth floor; the womens room is down the hall. | **5** My school's music room is decorated from floor to ceiling with ♪'s. | **6** Her brother-in-laws dog is smaller than my sister-in-laws cat. |
| **7** Are there any ATMs around here? | **8** Abdulkareem and Wildan's house is in Iraq. | **9** The banker's tie is decorated with dozens of $'s. |

Just for FUN!

Fix the sentences that are not punctuated correctly by putting apostrophes where they belong.

 *Professor Grammar's Punctuation Packets* • © 2011 by Marvin Terban • Scholastic Teaching Resources

**Name:** _____

**Date Due:** _____

# Quotation Marks

Quotations marks go around words to make them stand out from the rest of the sentence. Words that belong in quotation marks are direct quotes (the exact words someone has said), certain titles (songs, poems, chapters in a book, articles in newspapers or magazines, etc.), words used in unexpected ways, and definitions of words.

Quotation marks are small but really important. Here is a sentence without quotation marks:

> In the song Moo-zik for the Barnyard, the cow sings, Je t'adore, which means I love you in French, and the horse gets mad because he thinks the cow said, Shut the door.

How confusing! Let's put in the quotation marks and see how much easier it is to read the sentence.

> In the song "Moo-zik for the Barnyard," the cow sings, "Je t'adore," which means "I love you" in French, and the horse gets mad because he thinks she said, "Shut the door."

## Quotation marks help us by

✔ enclosing someone's exact words at the beginning, middle, or end of a sentence

✔ enclosing people's exact words when their words are split up

✔ identifying the titles of songs, poems, chapter titles, articles in newspapers or magazines, etc.

✔ pointing out words that are used in unexpected ways

✔ enclosing definitions and explanations in a sentence

In this packet, you'll learn several uses of quotation marks by doing fun activities and word games.

---

**Check off each activity page after you finish it.**

- [ ] 1. Quotation Marks: direct quotes at the start or end of a sentence
- [ ] 2. Quotation Marks: direct quotes, mid-sentence
- [ ] 3. Quotation Marks: quotes that are broken into parts
- [ ] 4. Quotation Marks: titles—songs, poems, articles, chapters, etc.
- [ ] 5. Quotation Marks: unfamiliar and unexpected words
- [ ] 6. Quotation Marks: definitions
- [ ] Quotation Marks Tic-Tac-Toe

# 1
# Quotation Marks

A direct quote tells the exact words that a person says. **Put quotation marks around a direct quote at the beginning or end of a sentence**, like this:

*"My computer just froze again,"* said Morgan.

Lucy suggested, *"Put it near the fireplace to warm it up."*

*"Very funny,"* thought Morgan.

Note: Sometimes even thoughts can be treated like direct quotes.

## Activity Directions

When investigating a crime, police detectives often have to ask people questions to find out what happened. Then they file reports with the responses people gave. One such report is below, but all the quotation marks that should go around what people said are missing. That's no good. That will make the report very hard to read. So grab a pencil and put in the missing quotation marks. You'll be helping the police.

---

OFFICIAL INVESTIGATION REPORT
## The Case of the Missing Science Project

I got the call at 10:15 a.m., Saturday morning.   My science project is missing! shouted a boy named David.

I'll be right over,  I said, and off I went.  I asked David,  Can you describe it to me?

It's made up of a lot of fun stuff like wheels, and gears, and switches, and it lights up and rings bells,  he said.

When did you see it last?  I inquired.

The boy said,  Last night.  Jennifer, my kid sister, was playing with it.

So I asked Jennifer,  Do you know where it is?

Laughing, she pointed under her bed.  There!  she shouted.

David's sister liked playing with it so much, she didn't want him to take it to school.

Thanks for finding it,  said David's mother.

His father added,  David worked on it for a month.

I'm glad I could help,  I answered.

I'll be more careful next time,  David said.

His little sister gurgled,  Bye, bye.

As I left, I thought to myself,  Boy, I'm good,  and I am!

Signed: *Jeffrey Finder*

Chief Investigator

## 2
# Quotation Marks

**Punctuation Rule**

Put quotation marks around **a direct quote in the middle of a sentence.** A direct quote states the exact words a person said. Here's an example of a direct quote in the middle of a sentence:

*The cow said, "Mooooo!" and walked back into the barn.*

### Activity Directions

Below is an interview with Lorrie Missouri, a famous teen entertainer. The interview is supposed to appear in an entertainment magazine, but something went wrong at the printer. The quotation marks didn't print. You can save the day. Add the quotation marks so the magazine can go to press on schedule. Millions of readers will thank you. Whew!

## My Exclusive Interview With Lorrie Missouri
### by U. No Who

When I first met Ms. Missouri, I asked her, Who are your best friends in show business? and she thought for a moment.

Finally, she answered, I've known Jane Maine and Alexis Texas for a long time, but before she could say anything else, there was a knock on the dressing room door. Lorrie open it, exclaimed, I can't believe it! and started jumping up and down with joy.

I recognized the two young women entering the dressing room and inquired, Della Delaware and Candice Kansas, what are you doing here? but they ignored me and rushed to their friend Lorrie.

Lorrie stopped jumping for a moment and said, They are here to see me star in my new show, of course, and then she hugged her friends.

Della and Candice burst into big grins and announced together, We have a surprise for you, and right behind them I saw none other than Virginia Virginia and Georgia Georgia.

By now the dressing room was getting crowded with teen stars, so Lorrie suggested, Let's go outside for some fresh air, and they all ran out, leaving me behind.

And that, folks, is my exclusive interview with Lorrie Missouri. You won't read it in any other magazine.

# 3
# Quotation Marks

Put quotation marks around a "broken quote." A broken quote is a direct quote that's split into two parts, like this:

*"Because of the unexpected heat wave," the teacher announced, "the annual snowman contest has been canceled."*

As you can see, the direct quote is "broken" in the middle, where the writer tells who is speaking.

## Activity Directions

The quotations below were spoken or written by famous people. Each one has been printed as a broken quote, with the name of the speaker identified in the middle of the quotation. Put quotation marks around the exact words the people said. That means you'll have to use in two pairs of quotation marks for each quote.

1.  To be or not to be,  said Hamlet,  that is the question.

2.  Think of all the beauty still left around you,  Anne Frank wrote in her diary, and be happy.

3.  History will be kind to me,  remarked Winston Churchill,  for I intend to write it.

4.  I have failed many times,  Michael Jordan admitted,  and that's why I am a success.

5.  If you tell the truth,  advised Mark Twain,  you don't have to remember anything.

6.  A slip of the foot you may soon recover,  wrote Benjamin Franklin, but a slip of the tongue you may never get over.

7.  Keep your face to the sunshine, Helen Keller recommended, and you cannot see the shadow.

8.  We must learn to live together as brothers,  said Martin Luther King, Jr.,  or perish together as fools.

9.  It is not fair to ask of others, wrote Eleanor Roosevelt, what you are unwilling to do yourself.

10. I never ran my train off the track, Harriet Tubman declared,  and I never lost a passenger.

# 4

# Quotation Marks

## Activity Directions

Below are some homework assignments. Everything is perfect except for the quotation marks. They're missing! Please add them where they belong according to the rule at right.

**Punctuation Rule**

Put quotation marks around the titles of songs, poems, articles in newspapers and magazines, chapters in books, TV show episodes, essays, short stories, short plays, speeches, and works of art.

Here are some examples:

Martin Luther King, Jr.'s "I Have a Dream" speech is one of the greatest ever made.

My favorite song from *The Lion King* is "Hakuna Matata."

Note: The titles of books, newspapers, magazines, movies, and TV shows should be <u>underlined</u> (when written by hand) or *italicized* (when typed on a computer).

## TONIGHT'S HOMEWORK

**MUSIC:** Learn the song A Night to Remember from *High School Musical 3* to sing at the talent show.

**ART HISTORY:** Find out why Leonardo da Vinci's painting Mona Lisa is also called La Gioconda.

**LITERATURE:** Read the chapter called Castle in the Air from *The Phantom Tollbooth.*

**SCIENCE:** Watch the episode called Your Nose on *The Amazing Human Body* tonight at 8:00 p.m. on Channel 66, and be sure to take notes.

**JOURNALISM:** Interview a teacher and write an article for the school newspaper called My Teacher's Favorite Things.

**ART:** Find pictures online of the famous statue The Thinker by Auguste Rodin and think about it.

**PLAYWRITING:** Write a short play called Nobody Will Believe This that begins with the sentence, "Nobody will believe this."

**POETRY:** Underline all the words you don't know in the poem When Cats Bark from the book *Animal Poetry*.

**PUBLIC SPEAKING:** Watch the video of a speech Barack Obama gave called The American Promise and find out what the promise is.

# 5

# Quotation Marks

## Activity Directions

You sometimes hear interesting things people say on a bus, train, or even an elevator. You're not eavesdropping. They're just talking loudly. Below are some comments overheard on a bus. Please add quotation marks according to the rule at right.

## Punctuation Rule

Put quotation marks around words or short phrases that are used in special, unusual, or peculiar ways. These words could be sarcastic, slang, ironic (the opposite of what you expect), funny, or they could even be nicknames.

Here are some examples:

Sarcastic: *I was still hungry after I ate that "huge" dinner my aunt promised me.*

Nickname: *Because he jumped so high, Michael Jordan was called "Air" Jordan.*

Slang: *This campfire is "cool."*

Ironic: *That tall kid blocking my view is called "Shorty."*

1. Wilt the Stilt Chamberlain, the great basketball player, was over 7 feet tall.

2. Because a $100 bill has Ben Franklin's picture on it, some people call it a Benjamin.

3. After he failed all his exams, his friends started calling him The Brain, but he didn't like the joke.

4. She rented a furnished apartment over the phone, but it had only a window shade and shower curtain.

5. President Eisenhower was called Ike, and President Lincoln was known as Honest Abe.

6. The so-called food they serve at the cafeteria tastes like cardboard and rubber.

7. My brother wouldn't go to that movie with us because he thought it was a chick flick.

8. The free sample I ordered online cost over $10 for shipping and handling!

9. The new student from England says we're his mates, calls gym shoes plimsolls, and goes on holiday when we take our vacation.

10. That easy test the teacher promised had 100 hard questions!

 *Professor Grammar's Punctuation Packets* • © 2011 by Marvin Terban • Scholastic Teaching Resources

# 6

# Quotation Marks

## Activity Directions

Help write the script for what happened on a TV quiz show called *Weird Words*. Two contestants competed against each other to define words and win prizes. Please put quotations marks around the definitions. (Hint: There are seven definitions below.) It may be hard to believe, but every one of the weird words on this page is real.

### Punctuation Rule

Put quotation marks around **definitions**, like this:

When you *twiddle* your fingers, you "twist or turn them absent-mindedly."

My Latin teacher says *carpe diem* means "seize the day."

Note: The word that is being defined is usually put in italics, like this: *arachnophobia* ("fear of spiders"). Foreign words are always italicized whether they are being defined or not: *Blumen* ("flowers" in German).

QUIZMASTER:  Contestant #1, your first word is *arglebargle.*

CONTESTANT 1:  Oh, that's easy.  *Arglebargle* means an argument.

CONTESTANT 2:  No, it doesn't.

CONTESTANT 1:  Yes, it does!

QUIZMASTER:  Let's not have an arglebargle about it.

CONTESTANT #2:  This show is giving me collywobbles.

QUIZMASTER:  What are those?

CONTESTANT #1:  *Collywobbles* means stomach pains.

CONTESTANT #2: That's because you're trying to bamboozle me, and *bamboozle* means to cheat somebody.

CONTESTANT #1:  I won't stand for this jiggery-pokery any more.

QUIZMASTER:  *Jiggery-pokery* means dishonest behavior, folks.

CONTESTANT #2:  I'm totally flabbergasted!

QUIZMASTER:  That means astonished. And so am I.  I've got to end this kerfuffle (that's a commotion or ruckus) immediately.

CONTESTANT #1: This is worse than a kerfuffle.  It's a brouhaha!

CONTESTANT #2:  I know that word.  *Brouhaha* means a kerfuffle.

QUIZMASTER:  I've had enough of this arglebargle, jiggery-pokery, kerfuffle, and brouhaha.  I'm getting collywobbles, too.  I'm going home.

# Punctuation
# Tic-Tac-Toe   Quotation Marks

Which of the sentences below have all the quotation marks where they should be? Mark each correct sentence by putting an X in the little checkbox. Get three Xs in a row and you win! Tic-Tac-Toe can be vertical, horizontal, or diagonal. Hint: There are two ways of winning the game below.

| | | |
|---|---|---|
| **1** "Don't forget to walk the goat after dinner," said his mother. ☐ | **2** He shouted, "This is the greatest thing that ever happened to me!" ☐ | **3** "I would if I could," she yelled, "but I can't, so I won't." ☐ |
| **4** I never knew that *hullabaloo* means a hubbub, which means an excited fuss. Did you? ☐ | **5** Someone ripped out an article from this magazine entitled "Don't Rip Out This Article." ☐ | **6** I thought I lost my cell phone, said my father, but it was right on the table where I left it. ☐ |
| **7** I liked all the poems in this book except the one called The Mouse in the House. ☐ | **8** My British cousin calls the elevator a "lift." ☐ | **9** Because he has a lot of allergies, we call my brother Sneezy. ☐ |

**Just for FUN!**

Fix the sentences that are not punctuated correctly by putting in quotation marks where they belong.

*Professor Grammar's Punctuation Packets* • © 2011 by Marvin Terban • Scholastic Teaching Resources

Name:_____

Date Due: _____

# Colons and Semicolons

A colon is a period on top of another period (:).
A semicolon is a period on top of a comma (;). They're cute punctuation marks—and very handy. Use a colon before a summary, list, or explanation. A colon is also used in the greeting of a business letter, for dialogue in scripts, and to show time (6:45 p.m.). A semicolon connects related, independent clauses, and separates items in a list when the list already has commas.

This sentence definitely needs colons and semicolons.

> At 1153 a.m., I had something important to do send e-mails to Ionia, Iowa Oxford, Ohio and Alta, Utah however, my computer was broken.

Colons and semicolons make it much easier to read.

> At 11:53 a.m., I had something important to do: send e-mails to Ionia, Iowa; Oxford, Ohio; and Alta, Utah; however, my computer was broken.

## Colons help us by

✔ introducing lists, summaries, and explanations

✔ making information, such as in memos, clearer

✔ punctuating the greeting in a business letter; addressing people in bulletins, warnings, instructions, and so on.

✔ separating hours from minutes in time and characters from dialogue in scripts

## Semicolons help us by

✔ connecting main clauses in a sentence—with and without conjunctions

✔ separating groups of words in a series (that already has commas)

In this packet, you'll learn several uses of colons and semicolons by doing fun activities and word games.

## Check off each activity page after you finish it.

☐ I. Colons: lists, explanations; memos

☐ 2. Colons: business letters; bulletins, warnings, etc.

☐ 3. Colons: to show time; in scripts and screenplays

☐ 4. Semicolons: to connect main clauses in a compound sentence

☐ 5. Semicolons: before certain conjunctions and phrases

☐ 6. Semicolons: between groups of words with commas in them

☐ Colons & Semicolons Tic-Tac-Toe

# 1

# Colons

## Activity Directions

Below is an important memo that's got to be sent out right away to the employees of a company. But all the colons are missing, and some people might not understand the memo. Please put in all the colons where they belong.

(HINT: 12 colons are missing from the memo.)

## Punctuation Rule

Use a colon after a complete sentence to introduce a list, an explanation, an example, or a definition.

*Bring these things to the pig-racing contest: a flag, a whistle, and pigs.*

*After studying for hours, he finally learned the definition of gallimaufry: a stew made of leftovers.*

**Use a colon after each heading in a memo.** What follows each colon helps define or explain the heading.

*To: Marcy*

*From: Terry*

*Date: Dec. 3, 2011*

*Subject: Our Next Business Trip*

To All Employees
From The New Boss
Subject About Me
Date Today

Many of you have asked me to tell you about myself, so here goes

I have five dogs Winston, Woodrow, Wilson, Waylon, and Sam.

I enjoy the following activities after work going home and taking a nap.

My favorite foods all begin with *k* kumquats, kiwi, knishes, and kale—all covered in ketchup.

I have a great theory about eating Start with dessert because you might be too full for it at the end of the meal.

Here are the names you can call me Mr. Muffin, Sam, or Boss.

The best lesson I ever learned in my life was this Don't try to whistle while eating crackers and peanut butter.

After just one day on this job, I have come to this conclusion I like it here!

# 2
# Colons

## Activity Directions
Below are several business letters and some signs that give instructions or orders. Please add the colons where they belong.

### Punctuation Rules

Use a colon after the greeting in a formal letter or business letter, like this:

*To the Bigger Banana Bureau:*

*Dear Dancing Dog Department:*

Use a colon after the name, title, or description of the person or persons being addressed in signs, instructions, bulletins, warnings, and so on.

*PASSENGERS: Have your tickets out and ready to hand in as you approach the gate.*

---

Dear Clean Air Committee

Will it make the air in my house healthier if I try to grow a tree in my bedroom?

Sincerely yours,

Marcy

---

Vegetarians

Our "hot dogs" contain no meat, and our "chicken salad" contains no chicken, so happy eating!

The Management

---

To Whom It May Concern

Don't sit on park benches after a rainstorm. Your pants will get wet.

The Parks Dept.

---

To All Pet Owners

No boa constrictors, alligators, or poisonous spiders allowed in school. That's the rule!

School Safety Committee

---

Dear Vegetable Association

This is to let you know that a tomato is not a vegetable. It is a fruit. It's true. Look it up.

Please correct your records.

Gratefully,

Hussein

---

All Clowns

Make sure to remove your red noses and green wigs before you take the bus home after the circus. You're freaking people out.

Thank you.

Freaked-Out Bus Riders

---

To the Office of Proper Dress

We don't think it's fair that we can't wear stripes and polka-dots together just because it makes you feel dizzy.

Ms. Youngman's Class

---

Dear Repair Department

Thanks for fixing my robot. However, it's broken again. The lawn mower ran over it. Do you think that made it stop working?

Yours truly,

Peter

# 3

# Colons

## Activity Directions

Below is the script for a scene in a movie. A crime has been committed, and the detective is questioning witnesses. It's important for her to determine the exact time of the crime. Help her out by putting colons where they belong. Thirty-one of them have mysteriously disappeared.

## Punctuation Rules

Use a colon to separate the hour from the minutes when you write out time, like this:
*He was born at exactly 12:43 a.m.*

In the script of a play or movie, use a colon to separate the name of a character from the words he or she says.

*Superman:* Up, up, and away!

*Lois:* He sure sounds a lot like Clark Kent.

## WHAT TIME DID THE LIGHTS GO OUT?

### Scene Three. The Detective is questioning witnesses in the drawing room.

Detective At what time did all the lights go out?

Witness 1  623 a.m.

Witness 2  No, it was 713 a.m.

Witness 3  I disagree. It was more like 833 a.m.

Detective  Well, what time did they go back on?

Witness 1  Sometime between 953 a.m. and 1043 a.m.

Witness 2  No, no. It was much closer to 840 a.m.

Witness 3  I disagree again. It was much later. Probably around 1150 a.m.

Detective  Well, what time was lunch served?

Witness 1  The same time it always is. 1230 p.m.

Witness 3  I disagree again. I didn't get my lunch until 115. I was starving!

Detective  Well, that solves the case.

Witnesses 1, 2, and 3  What case?

Detective  The case of when the lights went out!

Witnesses 1, 2, and 3  Well, when did they go out?

Detective  At exactly 747 a.m.

Witnesses 1, 2, and 3  How did you discover that?

Detective  It was on the news. There was a blackout at that moment all over the city.

Witnesses 1, 2, and 3  You're brilliant!

Detective  I know. And modest, too. Oh, it's 426 p.m. I have to get back to the station.

# 4
# Semicolons

## Activity Directions

Here are a bunch of independent clauses (clauses that can be sentences by themselves). They have been put together to make compound sentences. A semicolon is needed to hold the clauses together; please put them in where they belong.

### Punctuation Rule

Use a semicolon to connect related main clauses in a compound sentence if there's no conjunction (linking word).

A **clause** is a group of words with a subject and a verb. A **main clause** could be a sentence by itself. A **compound sentence** is made up of main clauses that are related in meaning. Here are some examples.

Sentence 1: *His sister collects rocks.*
Sentence 2: *He likes to read.*
Compound sentence: *His sister collects rocks; he likes to read.*

Note: This sentence could also be written as *His sister collects rocks, and he likes to read.* A semicolon can sometimes take the place of a comma and a conjunction.

Here's another example of a semicolon connecting clauses:

*It snowed all through the night; in the morning we made snowpeople in the field.*

---

**1.** Her uncle is a butcher + her aunt makes the hamburgers =
Her uncle is a butcher her aunt makes the hamburgers.

**2.** It rains a lot here in April + it's great for growing flowers =
It rains a lot here in April it's great for growing flowers.

**3.** Grandpa looks great with his beard + he should have grown it years ago =
Grandpa looks great with his beard he should have grown it years ago.

**4.** It's been raining for three days + it's great weather for ducks =
It's been raining for three days it's great weather for ducks.

**5.** She's been studying astronomy + she loves the stars =
She's been studying astronomy she loves the stars.

**6.** Everest is the highest mountain on Earth + Cotahuasi, in Peru, is the deepest canyon
= Everest is the highest mountain on Earth Cotahuasi, in Peru, is the deepest canyon.

**7.** A hamburger has no ham in it + a hot dog is not a dog =
A hamburger has no ham in it a hot dog is not a dog.

# 5
# Semicolons

**Punctuation Rule**

Put a semicolon in front of the following conjunctions and phrases when they join clauses together.

| | |
|---|---|
| accordingly | in addition |
| also | in fact |
| as a result | indeed |
| besides | moreover |
| consequently | nevertheless |
| for example | on the contrary |
| for this reason | on the other hand |
| furthermore | that is |
| hence | therefore |
| however | thus |

Note: Always put a comma *after* these conjunctions and phrases.

## Activity Directions

Some fairy tale characters have sent text messages to other fairy tale characters. They've used some of the conjunctions and phrases from the list at right, but they forgot to put in semicolons where they belong. That's your job. Add one semicolon to each text message below.

Little Red Riding Hood to the Big Bad Wolf:
You ate my grandmother as a result,
I'm not your friend.

Big Bad Wolf to Little Red Riding Hood:
People think I'm mean on the contrary,
I'm a nice guy. Really.

Goldilocks to The Three Bears:
I slept in your beds in addition, I ate your
porridge. Sorry.

Snow White to the Seven Dwarfs:
I'm a great housekeeper for example, I can
clean, cook, and sew.

Big Bad Wolf to the Three Little Pigs:
I'll huff and I'll puff in fact, I'll blow your
houses down.

Little Miss Muffet to the Spider:
You frightened me away nevertheless,
I'm coming back for my curds and whey.

Prince Charming to Cinderella:
Your foot fit the glass slipper for this reason,
I'll marry you.

Beauty to the Beast:
You are a beast on the other hand, beasts
can be lovable, too.

Hansel to Gretel:
It's getting dark moreover, we're lost in the
woods. Yikes!

Jill to Jack:
Let's go up the hill again however, don't
fall down this time.

*Professor Grammar's Punctuation Packets* • © 2011 by Marvin Terban • Scholastic Teaching Resources

# 6
# Semicolons

## Activity Directions

Below is the poster for a three-ring circus that announces who will be performing in each ring. The sentences are confusing because there are no semicolons to separate the groups of words. Please put them in so the circus-goers will know who is performing in each ring.

## Punctuation Rule

Use a semicolon between groups of words in a series that already have commas in them, like this:

*The singers were from Chelsea, Massachusetts; Brooklyn, New York; and Dallas, Texas.*

*At the pet store, Martin bought bird seeds, a fish tank, and a gerbil cage; at the supermarket, he got eggs, bananas, and milk; and at the computer store, he got a printer, a flash drive, and blank DVDs.*

## In Ring 1

**You'll love . . .**

Paula Paws, the animal trainer, and her dancing bear, Twinkletoes  Mr. Stretch, the world's tallest man, and his little dog, Pooch and Blaze and Flame, the fire-eating frogs.

## In Ring 2

**You'll cheer for . . .**

Swing and Sway, the daredevil trapeze artists Boom, the human cannonball and Chewy, the fearless man who sticks his head in a lion's mouth.

## In Ring 3

**You'll laugh at . . .**

Mr. Fingers, who juggles bubbles, feathers, and water Frosting and Crumbs, the pie-throwing dogs and Henny, the singing chicken.

# Punctuation
# Tic-Tac-Toe

Colons and Semicolons

Which of the sentences below have the colons and semicolons in the right places? Mark each correct sentence by putting an X in the little checkbox. Get three Xs in a row and you win! Tic-Tac-Toe can be vertical, horizontal, or diagonal. Hint: There are two ways of winning the game below.

| | | |
|---|---|---|
| **1** Father  How did you do on your report card?<br><br>Son  Like Abraham Lincoln.<br><br>Father What do mean?<br><br>Son  I went down in history. | **2** Take these items to the yard sale: your old CDs, your dad's typewriter, and the green hula hoops. | **3** To The Sales Dept.<br><br>From Customer Service<br><br>Date Aug. 14, 2010<br><br>Subject The New Can Opener<br><br>It doesn't work! |
| **4** The chicken played the piano the rabbit danced. | **5** The day was beautiful: sunny, warm, and breezy. | **6** Ticket holders<br><br>Line up single file. Don't push! |
| **7** To the members of Congress:<br><br>Hello there.<br><br>Jimmy | **8** If you leave at 7:45 a.m., and there's no traffic, you'll get to school by 8:10 a.m., at the latest. | **9** The dam burst and flooded the town; consequently, the parade was canceled. |

**Just for FUN!**

Fix the sentences that are not punctuated correctly by putting in the colons and semicolons where they belong.

 *Professor Grammar's Punctuation Packets* • © 2011 by Marvin Terban • Scholastic Teaching Resources

# Answer Key

## Commas I

### Commas 1 (p. 8)

1. Six of the longest rivers in the world are the Nile in Africa, **C**ongo in Central Africa, **L**ena in Russia, **A**mazon in South America, **M**ississippi in the USA, and the Yangtze in China. Answer: *clam*

2. Earth, **J**upiter, **U**ranus, **M**ars, **P**luto (a dwarf planet), **S**aturn, and Neptune are some of the planets in our solar system. Answer: He *jumps*.

3. William Shakespeare wrote many great plays like Hamlet, **K**ing Lear, **O**thello, **A**s You Like It, **L**ove's Labours Lost, **a**nd Macbeth. Answer: *koala*

4. Goslings, **s**quabs, **h**atchlings, **e**phynas, **e**yases, **p**olliwogs, and fawns are the names of baby geese, pigeons, dinosaurs, jellyfish, hawks, frogs, and deer. Answer: *sheep*

5. Some of the instruments in an orchestra are violins, **h**orns, **o**boes, **o**rgans, **f**lutes, **s**axophones, and drums. Answer: *hoofs*

6. My favorite animated movies are *Up*, *Ratatouille*, *Alice in Wonderland*, *Bambi*, *Beauty and the Beast*, *Ice Age*, *Toy Story*, *Shrek*, and *Happy Feet*. Answer: *rabbits*

### Commas 2 (p. 9)

1. My brother really doesn't like peanut butter and mushroom sandwiches.

2. My goodness, **r**abbits can hop fast when they want to.

3. Gosh, **a**ll my licorice melted in the sun.

4. Yuck, **c**otton candy really sticks to your face, doesn't it?

5. My dear friend from camp is visiting this weekend.

6. Uh-oh, **e**verybody just went out the wrong door.

7. Oops, **C**arl squirted ketchup on my new shirt.

8. Oh dear, **a** page from my homework just blew out the window.

9. Gee whiz, **r**accoons broke into the kitchen and ate Grandma's apple pie.

Answer: *racecar* or *race car*

### Commas 3 (p. 10)

Dear Grandma,

Although I've been here for only one week, I've already made a lot of new friends. Because kids come here from my school, I knew some of them already. Since this camp is right on a lake, we do a lot of water sports, like swimming and boating. Unless it's really raining, we're outside all day long. After the swim across the lake, we had a picnic. Before the talent show yesterday, I had to practice singing with my mouth full of pretzels. I won for funniest act! If you can come on visiting day, that would be awesome. Until I see you again, stay well. Hug Fluffy for me.

Love,

Summer

### Commas 4 (p. 11)

1. When the mosquitoes came out, **i**n went the people.

2. While they were flying, **n**ine planes flew in front of them.

3. Outside the bedroom, **c**arpet the hallway.

4. Though we believe in recycling, **o**ur brother doesn't.

5. After you read the book, **r**eport on it to the class.

6. Please tell Paul, **R**evere is a city in Massachusetts.

7. When he began painting, **e**veryone said he needed art lessons.

8. To make ice, **c**hill water.

9. Before they finished eating, **the** chicken flew away.

10. To Abraham, **L**incoln seemed like a good capital for Nebraska.

11. Inside, **y**our grandpa's barn was noisy.

Answer: *incorrectly*

### Commas 5 (p. 12)

Dear President Washington,
Sincerely yours,

Dear President Grant,
Yours truly,

Dear President Garfield,
Your friend,

Dear President Jefferson,
Respectfully,

Dear President Obama,
Be well,

Dear President Lincoln,
Best wishes,

### Commas 6 (p. 13)

What is full of holes, Amanda, but stills holds water? A sponge, Justin.

Which weighs more, Steve, a pound of feathers or a pound of iron? Jane, they both weigh a pound.

Why didn't the skeleton go to the dance, Sophie? Because, Matt, he had no body to go with.

Dennis, why did Dracula's mother get him cough medicine? Because of his coffin, Lynda.

### Commas I Tic-Tac-Toe (p. 14)

1. My favorite authors are J. K. Rowling, Dr. Seuss, Maurice Sendak, and Judy Blume. ☒

2. Gosh, I never knew our teacher could sing opera like that.

3. When the stage lights came on, on came the jugglers. ☒

4. You can't bring an alligator to school, Roslyn, even if he is your best friend!

5. Hello, everyone, and welcome to the zoo. ☒

6. Dear Harriet, Come visit me in Vermont.
Love, Len ☒

7. I told George, Washington is both a city and a state.

8. Pitch the tent, gather logs, open the sleeping bags, and then we'll camp out.

9. Since it's raining so hard, we'll have to postpone the pig races. ☒

# Commas II

## Commas 1 (p. 16)

Lorraine's Luscious Lemons & Limes: Fresh, Juicy Fruits—right off the tree

Shana's Shoes: Stylish, Chic, Affordable Footwear for Those Special Nights Out

Ed & Esther's Electronics: The latest, greatest, most amazing, new gadgets in stock!

Karen's Kids' Clothing: Darling, Adorable, Delightful Fashions for Your Children

Barbara's Bed & Bath: Puffy, Fluffy Towels and Smooth, Soft Sheets

Tiger's Terrific Toys: Lovable, Huggable Bears to Be Your Best Friends

Jen's Jewels: Gorgeous, Sparkling, Elegant Rings and Bracelets

Freedman's Furniture: Comfortable, durable sofas to make your home more livable

Lorrie's Lovely Lollipops: flavorful, juicy treats on sticks

Roslyn's Restaurant: Tasty, Scrumptious, Delectable Dishes to Please Your Taste Buds

Lexi's Linens: Elegant, Exclusive, Luxurious Bedspreads and Comforters for a Great Night's Sleep

Harriet's Hats: Fabulous, Fashionable, Feathered Chapeaus for Those Special Occasions

## Commas 2 (p. 17)

It rained on Monday, snowed on Tuesday, but was nice on Wednesday.

Gerry has a cat, Lynette has a dog, and I have a canary.

The hamburger was delicious, the hot dog was tasty, and the dessert was great.

Justin could ride his bike to school, he could take the bus, or he could walk.

The horse neighed loudly, the kitten purred softly, but the pig didn't say a thing.

At the party, Margo recited a poem, Mike played the guitar, and Max told jokes.

## Commas 3 (p. 18)

1. Marion Moon was the mother of Buzz Aldrin, the second man on the moon.

2. Vincent van Gogh, the famous painter, sold only one painting in his whole life – to his brother!

3. Marie Curie, the first woman to win a Nobel Prize, won it twice!

4. Bill Gates, the computer genius, wrote his first computer program at thirteen.

5. Samuel Langhorn Clemens was the real name of Mark Twain, the author of *Tom Sawyer*.

6. General George Custer, the youngest man ever to become a general in the U.S. Army, graduated last in his class at West Point.

7. Sally Ride, the first American woman to ride into space, answered a newspaper ad looking for people who wanted to be astronauts.

8. Shirley Chisholm, an African-American congresswoman from New York, ran for president in 1972.

9. John Quincy Adams, president of the U.S. from 1825 to 1829, kept a pet alligator in the White House.

10. Isabella Baumfree was the birth name of Sojourner Truth, the American abolitionist in the 1800s.

11. Charles Dickens, the author of *Oliver Twist*, slept facing north because he thought it improved his writing.

12. Sandra Day O'Connor, the first woman on the Supreme Court, has a school named after her in Phoenix, Arizona.

## Commas 4 (p. 19)

1. These shoes, which are a size 8, don't match that dress.

2. A giraffe, which can stand as tall as 18 feet, cleans it ears with its tongue.

3. Balloons and cactus plants, as you can see, don't mix.

4. My grandfather, who is almost 90 years old, loves to climb trees.

5. Eat plenty of fruits, especially oranges, to be healthy.

6. Ms. Jannetta, not Ms. Allen, is my history teacher.

7. The Eiffel Tower, which opened in 1889, is in Paris, France.

8. The music, in my opinion, is way too loud.

## Commas 5 (p. 20)

This porpoise goes to 51 Grove Street, Jade, MN, on June 20, 2013, and don't drip water on the carpet when you carry it inside.

Mrs. Laurie at 6 Stoney Brook Lane, Glenn, ND, needs this rhinoceros no later than June 22, 2013, and don't stick yourself on its horn.

Rush this giraffe to 6 Ledgewood Way, Bonnie, NE, before February 14, 2013, and be careful going under bridges and overpasses.

The anteater must arrive at 39 Stanwood Road, Scottswamp, OH, on November 7, 2011, and take this jar of ants along for snacks.

On December 4, 2012, carry this hippo to 1610 Lenox Ave., Dylan, FL, and you'd better take a few extra men with you.

Make sure this shipment of alligators gets to 99 Avenue B, Summy, IL, by July 22, 2012, and don't stick your fingers in the cage.

Dispatch these butterflies to 66 Madison Avenue, Edward, MS, by August 28, 2012, and never open the carton to look in.

Transport this bald eagle to 5 Greenbriar Road, Howard, TX, by December 19, 2011, and don't muss its hair.

Professor Grammar's Punctuation Packets • © 2011 by Marvin Terban • Scholastic Teaching Resources

This peacock goes to 2100 Shumard Oak Lane, Irving, MA, by November 5, 2011, and be careful of its feathers.

Send this kangaroo to 12 Cottonwood Avenue, Judi, NY, no later than March 12, 2012, and don't let it jump around too much.

### Commas 6 (p. 21)

I asked Ms. Konokowski, the math teacher, what her favorite food was. She answered, "Chocolate covered worms, of course."

Mrs. Scotto, another math teacher, said her favorite people were her grandsons. "Matt and David," she stated, "are cuter than worms."

Mrs. Millan, the lady in the corner office, loves the environment. "*Clean Up the World* is the best TV show," she declared.

Mr. Greenblatt, the substitute teacher, stated, "My favorite animal is Madison,, my cat, because she sleeps with me each night."

Ms. Soares, the language teacher, said, "My favorite movie is *Vampires Eat New Jersey*. I watch it all the time."

When I asked Ms. Cho, the school nurse, what her favorite color was, she answered, "Chartreuse," and then she added, "with a slight touch of magenta."

### Commas II Tic-Tac-Toe (p. 22)

1. The giant cucumber, which I found on the subway, grows in only one place in the world: a tiny island near Hawaii.

2. My darling granddaughter was born on June 22, 2007, in New York, NY.

3. Take this money, jump on your bike, ride to the store, and get me a dozen worms so that we can go fishing.

4. Mike shouted to Linda from the train window, "Don't forget the knishes!"

5. Aaron is a big, tall, handsome, smart, young man with a great sense of humor.

6. This *cornutia grandifolia* flower, which I got from a friend in Florida, attracts butterflies and hummingbirds.

7. She picked up the bat, walked up to the plate, swung fiercely at the ball, and hit a home run out of the park! ☒

8. Peach melba and melba toast, two foods I love, were named after Nellie Melba, a famous opera singer. ☒

9. Arlene whispered, "I think I left Jack's porcupine on the school bus." ☒

## Capital Letters I

### Capital Letters 1 (p. 24)

1. **T**alking very softly, she said, "**L**ove your porcupine, but don't hug it."
   TLC (Tender Loving Care)

2. **D**on't ever say, "**V**ampire bats are cute," in my house!
   DVD (Digital Video Disc)

3. **V**ery often my aunt would shout, "**I**ce is cold!"
   VIP (Very Important Person)

4. **R**ecently they announced, "**I**gloos don't make good homes in the desert."
   RIP (Rest in Peace)

5. **I**nside the mountain, the caveman was singing, "**R**ocks really rock!"
   IRS (Internal Revenue Service)

6. **U**ncle George mumbled, "**F**eathers tickle," and then he sneezed.
   UFO (Unidentified Flying Object)

7. **N**ow I'm going to tell her, "**F**lamingos don't belong in the kitchen."
   NFL (National Football League)

8. **F**ortunately Grandma whispered, "**B**ananas are sometimes green."
   FBI (Federal Bureau of Investigation)

### Capital Letters 2 (p. 25)

1. My cousin, **G**eorgio **I**ngelbert from **R**ussia, met his girlfriend, **A**lberta **F**eather, in **F**rance on top of the **E**iffel Tower. GIRAFFE

2. On my tour, I went to **E**dinburgh and **L**ondon (where they speak **E**nglish), then to **P**aris, **H**avana, **A**msterdam (in the **N**etherlands), and **T**okyo. ELEPHANT

3. **A**lbert **L**ong moved from **L**ong **I**sland to **G**eorgia, and then to **A**bilene, **T**exas, where he ate popcorn made by **O**rville **R**edenbacher. ALLIGATOR

4. In **H**amburg, **I**owa, **P**enelope **P**epper sent an e-mail to her friend in **O**rlando. HIPPO

5. **M**ax **O**blong, from **N**etawaka, **K**entucky, married his girlfriend, **E**dith, while jumping out of a plane over **Y**onkers. MONKEY

6. The **S**wiss man who drank **T**urkish coffee swam the **A**mazon **R**iver, while his friend **F**red walked from **I**reland to **S**weden speaking **H**indi! STARFISH

7. My cousins went to three colleges: **M**iami **U**niversity, Loyola, and **E**merson. MULE

8. In **H**ungary, the names of actual cities are **I**brany, **N**agyatad, and **N**agykanizsa, but not **Y**psilanti, which is in another place entirely. HINNY

### Capital Letters 3 (p. 26)

Wednesday, November 11
**V**eterans Day

Monday, January 26
**A**sian Lunar New Year

Monday, September 7
**L**abor Day

Saturday–Monday, September 19–21
Eid-al-Fitr

Thursday, December 31
**N**ew Year's Eve

Tuesday, July 4
**I**ndependence Day

Tuesday, **N**ovember 3
**E**lection Day

Sunday, April 4
Easter

Friday, June 22
**D**og and Cat Appreciation Day

Friday, April 23
**A**rbor Day

Monday, September 28
**Y**om Kippur

Heartfelt Holiday:
*Valentine's Day*

## Capital Letters 4 (p. 27)

1. Tylenol Wheaties Iams Nike Spalding
Baseball team: Baltimore TWINS

2. Benetton Rayovac Alpo Vaseline Exxon Subaru
Baseball team: Atlanta BRAVES

3. Macy's Ebay Toyota Sunkist
Baseball team: New York METS

4. Alka Seltzer Tums Rolex Olympus Scholastic
Baseball team: Houston ASTROS

5. Crayola Uniroyal Buick Starkist
Baseball team: Chicago CUBS

6. Rubbermaid Energizer Dell Samsung
Baseball team: Cincinnati REDS

7. Geico Ihop Amazon.com Nintendo Texaco Sears
Baseball team: San Francisco GIANTS

8. Pampers Adidas Duracell Reebok Epson Starburst
Baseball team: San Diego PADRES

9. Maytag Applebee's Raisinettes Lipton Izod Nabisco Snickers
Baseball team: Florida MARLINS

10. Texas Instruments General Electric Radio Shack
Baseball team: Detroit TIGERS

## Capital Letters 5 (p. 28)

1. *How to Amuse the Whiskers of a Kitten:* HAWK

2. "Give Us Lots of Love": GULL

3. *Terror Everywhere! Right Now!:* TERN

4. *Octopuses, Walruses, and Lizards:* OWL

5. "Let's All Raid the Kitchen": LARK

6. *Dragons and Unicorns Can't Kiss:* DUCK

7. *Judo, Acrobatics, and Yoga:* JAY

8. "Castles of Raindrops on the Ocean of Wonder": CROW

9. *Kentucky Independent World Inquirer:* KIWI

10. *Weird Reptiles and Eerie Nests:* WREN

## Capital Letters 6 (p. 29)

1. Last night on **Hopping Around the Globe**, I watched "Inside **I**ndia" and "**T**ouring **I**celand." HAITI

2. I'm reading two great books: **P**ickles **E**verlasting and *A **R**ainy Day in **U**ruguay.* PERU

3. **K**aren said, "**E**lephants don't live in **N**ew **Y**ork (except in zoos), **A**aron." KENYA

4. On my world tour, I ate **C**heerios in **U**ganda and Raisin **B**ran in **A**lbania. CUBA

5. **J**ennifer shouted to **A**lexandra, "**P**lease stop **A**ndrew from eating **N**ana's cookies!" JAPAN

6. In New York City, you can see to the top of the **E**mpire State Building, visit **G**rant's Tomb, go to a game at **Y**ankee Stadium, picnic in Central **P**ark, and gaze at the lights in **T**imes Square all in one day! EGYPT

7. **C**olumbus Day and **H**alloween are in the fall, **I**ndependence Day and **L**abor Day are in the summer, and **E**aster is in the spring. CHILE

8. We stayed at the **T**umbledown **I**nn and ate at **B**urrito **E**at-O! on **T**uesday. TIBET

## Capital Letters I Tic-Tac-Toe (p. 30)

1. If you ever meet my cousin, never ask her, "Do you like radishes?". ☒

2. Jennifer loves Japanese food, but David eats only Danish dishes. ☒

3. I saw a display of Cuisinart coffee makers at Macy's. ☒

4. Amazingly, the book *My Little Turtle* was made into the play *Petunias for Penelope*, then into the movie *Thunder on Miami.*

5. Six presidents of the United States were named James: Madison, Monroe, Polk, Buchanan, Garfield, and Carter. ☒

6. On my trip to Europe, I ate French food in France and Swiss cheese in Switzerland.

7. There are four or five Sundays in every March. ☒

8. I wrote a letter to the TV station when my favorite show, Monkeys From Mars, was taken off the air. ☒

9. The class jumped for joy when the teacher announced, "There will be no homework tonight!" ☒

# Capital Letters II

## Capital Letters 1 (p. 32)

Hello, Grandma,
We're in the **S**outh enjoying Florida, but we miss our relatives in the **N**orth, so we'll soon be driving north to see you. Miss ya!
Renae

Dear Georgia cousins,
It's pretty cold in the **N**orthwest today. I'll bet you're all nice and toasty in the **S**outheast. Brrrrr!
Your cousin from Oregon

Salutations, Mom and Dad,
I'm traveling east from the **M**idwest, so in a few days, I'll be back **E**ast and can visit you in Philadelphia. I'm having fun. Send money!
Your son, Dave

Dear Uncle Johnny,
We're flying west toward Nevada over the Rocky Mountains. Those things are tall!
See you soon,
Isla

What's up, guys?
We're camping out near the Grand Canyon in the **S**outhwest. That thing is deep!
Valentine

Dear Terri,
I'm visiting my grandparents in the great **N**ortheast this summer. Tomorrow we're driving south from Boston to Washington, D.C. I'll say "Hi!" to the president for you.
Pete

## Capital Letters 2 (p. 33)

Monday

8:00 to 9:00 p.m.: **M**edieval Times: What were the **M**iddle **A**ges in the middle of?

9:00 to 10:00 p.m.: The First Ten Amendments: Was the **B**ill of **R**ights right?

*Professor Grammar's Punctuation Packets* • © 2011 by Marvin Terban • Scholastic Teaching Resources

10:00 to 11:00 p.m.: Men in Armor: How hot and heavy were those **T**rojan **W**ar suits?

Tuesday

8:00 to 9:00 p.m.: When People Are Revolting: The **F**rench **R**evolution vs. the **A**merican **R**evolution

9:00 to 10:00 p.m.: The Great Charter: What the **M**agna **C**arta really says about King John

10:00 to 11:00 p.m.: Quill Pen: How Jefferson wrote the **D**eclaration of **I**ndependence without a computer

Wednesday

8:00 to 9:00 p.m.: Freeing the Slaves: We unlock the **E**mancipation **P**roclamation.

9:00 to 10:00 p.m.: North vs. South: What was civil about the **C**ivil **W**ar?

10:00 to 11:00 p.m.: Know-It-Alls: Were people smarter during the **R**enaissance just because they knew everything?

Thursday

8:00 to 9:00 p.m.: Brother, Can You Spare a Dime?: Why the **G**reat **D**epression wasn't so great!

9:00 to 10:00 p.m.: Mighty Metals: Was the **B**ronze **A**ge better than the **I**ron **A**ge?

10:00 to 11:00 p.m.: The Long, Long War: Why the **C**rusades lasted 200 years!

Friday

8:00 to 9:00 p.m.: You're Right!: What the **U**nited **S**tates **C**onstitution means to you.

9:00 to 10:00 p.m.: Breaking Up Is So Hard: The reasons for the **W**ar of **I**ndependence

10:00 to 11:00 p.m.: The **G**ettysburg **A**ddress: It isn't 1600 Pennsylvania Avenue.

## Capital Letters3 (p. 34)

To Joan of Arc:

My **D**ear Miss Arc,

I really admire you because you were shorter than I am and you still led an army.

**R**ock on,

Justin

To Ben Franklin:

**G**ood morning, Mr. Franklin,

Did you know what was going to happen when the lightning hit the key or were you shocked?

**S**incerely,

Jessica and Aaron

To Thomas Edison:

**H**ello, Mr. Edison,

Thanks for inventing the light bulb. I can read much better at night now.

**B**rightly yours,

Amanda

To William Shakespeare:

**H**ark, Will,

When my brother forgot our apartment number, he asked, "2B or not 2B?" I guess he got that from you.

**C**heerio,

Shana

To the Wright Brothers:

**G**reetings, Orville and Wilbur,

How come your first flight lasted only 120 feet? You could have just walked that far, right?

**O**ver and out,

Jade Leong

To Isaac Newton:

**K**ind Sir,

Is the Fig Newton named after you?

**Y**ours truly,

Sasha

## Capital Letters 4 (p. 35)

**P**resident Millard McKinley; **G**overnor Alphonse Mutter; **M**ayor Horatio Hopper; **S**enator Gilbert Moose; **K**ing Albert III; **L**ord Reginald Mountbatty; **D**uchess Frederica Fishy; **P**rime **M**inister Wallace Waffle

## Capital Letters 5 (p. 36)

Party List: **A**unt Shirley, **G**randpa Lester, and **C**ousin Sybil.

Tell **D**ad the dog buried the remote control in the backyard.

Jed, Please get **M**om some worms for her pet bird when you go to the market. Don't forget!

Did **G**randma give **G**randpa a motorcycle for his birthday? Cool!

Is **A**unt Olive bringing the hot dogs or the buns?

At 9 a.m., **G**ranny is going to be interviewed on the *Hello, Everyone!* show.

Find out if my grandfather made relish.

Remember to give **N**ana Rachel her umbrella with the bamboo handle.

## Capital Letters 6 (p. 37)

I was sailing west to find the **E**ast, but I bumped into a new world.

**B**est wishes,

**C**aptain C. Columbus

**D**ear anyone,

Help!

**S**incerely,

Lost at Sea

Inside this bottle is a copy of the **B**ill of **R**ights. Please pay the bill for it, okay?

I never liked the **D**uke of **W**ellington at the **B**attle of **W**aterloo.

Defeatedly,

**E**mperor Napoleon

Hi, **M**om and **D**ad,

I'm sailing northeast then southwest around the world. I won't be home for dinner.

**L**ove,

Richard

### Capital Letters II Tic-Tac-Toe (p. 38)

1. If you live in the Southwest, you'd better have a good air conditioner.

2. Every Easter, I love to make colorful eggs and roll them on the lawn. ☒

3. If you drive north for three days, you'll come to the cities of the Northeast.

4. In mythology class, we read about Apollo, the god of the sun, medicine, archery, poetry, dance, music, and other stuff. ☒

5. My dear friend,
   I hope you are well.
   Best wishes,
   Your secret admirer ☒

6. My favorite relative, Aunt Lorrie, always bakes the best chocolate chip cookies for Christmas. ☒

7. It was an honor to meet Mayor Millan and Governor Sanz yesterday.

8. Dinosaurs roamed the Earth during the Triassic and Jurassic periods. ☒

9. Before they were married, Mom and Dad had dated in high school.

## End Punctuation

### Question Marks 1 (p. 40)

What's your pet goat's name?

Where is your house?

Is he your dog?

What is that?

Is this your red umbrella, sir?

Does anyone know the way down to the field?

Can you describe the bird that stole your big hat?

Is the play going to start soon?

Who was the first president on a postage stamp?

If I lend you a dollar, will you pay it back soon?

Why did you say that to his favorite pet fish?

Mom, where was Grandfather born?

Is this the stop for the art museum?

Who is the man with the long coat?

Where did I hide my brother's hat?

Do you like my new blue sneakers?

Where will they go after that party?

**Note:** The question marks form a large "?"

### Exclamation Points 2 (p. 41)

What is that loud sound?

Run! it's an erupting volcano!

That was just my stomach rumbling.

A boa constrictor is crawling up my leg!

It's a killer snake from Central and South America.

How is that going to help me?

Is there a police station around here?

There's one next to the Italian pastry shop.

Help, someone stole my cannoli!

What act are you doing for the talent show?

I'm dressing up as a duck and singing opera.

That's amazingly fantastic!

I will not dance in the ballet tonight.

Why not, madam?

I refuse to wear that totally terrible tutu!

Here's the lion house at the zoo.

How are you feeling, lion?

Roar!

Do you hear that loud buzzing?

It's just a bumblebee.

Ow! It just stung my arm!

It's nice here in the woods.

Did you hear that scary noise?

It's Bigfoot!

Answer: O G I C U R M T (Oh, gee, I see you are empty!)

### Exclamation Points 3 (p. 42)

When Asta the astronaut flew into space,

The sky was pitch black and not blue.

She shouted out, "Wow! What a wonderful place!"

And "Oh! What a marvelous view!"

Hurray! Hurray! We won the prize!

The golden cup is ours!

The crowd yells, "Yeah! We love you guys! "

And showers us with flowers.

Eek! A mouse is in my house!

It ran across the floor!

But I won't have to call my spouse,

'Cause phew! It just flew out the door.

When Little Lord Lonny came down with the flu,

The doctor came over and said, "Drink this goo."

Lonny screamed, "Ugh! That stuff tastes just like glue! "

And "Ouch! That big needle you gave me hurt, too! "

### Periods 4 (p. 43)

The dinosaur is loose!

What should we do?

**3.** I am going to wave when it goes by.

Is today Wednesday?

**5.** It is.

Yikes, I forgot to study for the math test!

7. I like turpoljes.

What are they?

9. They're spotted pigs.

10. I spotted one once.

Why did you say that?

What did I say?

13. You said you like asparagus.

14. I do.

But why did you say it?

Help! Help!

What's the matter?

An earthquake is shaking the house!

19. That's just an elephant walking by.

20. Money doesn't grow on trees.

Then why do banks have branches?

**Add:** 3+5+7+9+10+13+14+19+20 = 100.
Answer: *The Roman numeral C stands for 100.*

## Periods 5 (p. 44)

The mild imperative sentences are:

1. **T**ake your purple umbrella today.
2. **R**aise your hand if you know the answer.
5. **O**pen your books to the chapter on tap-dancing frogs.
7. **U**nbutton the baby's coat when you go inside.
9. **B**efore you eat, wash your hands.
11. **L**et all the snakes out of their cages before you go home today.
12. **E**njoy yourself at the masquerade party.
13. **M**ove your baby dinosaur to the next cage.
14. **A**sk questions if you don't understand something.
16. **K**iss your kangaroo to show you love it.
18. **I**nsert tab A into slot B.
19. **N**ever say "Ish-ka-bibble" to me again, please.
22. **G**et all your stuff and follow me.

Answer: *troublemaking*

## Periods 6 (p. 45)
### Activity 1

Gen. Hickory Battle (General)

Rep. Reginald Law (Representative)

Sen. Phineas Filibuster (Senator)

Rev. Peter Pewter (Reverend)

Fred Feelgood, M. D. (Medical Doctor)

Jacob Jabber, Jr. (Junior)

### Activity 2

J. K. Rowling: Joanne Kathleen

J. R. R. Tolkien: John Ronald Reuel

C. S. Lewis: Clive Staples

### End Punctuation Tic-Tac-Toe (p. 46)

1. It is always colder in winter than in summer. ☒
2. Flee! Run! Escape! A spaceship full of monsters has just landed in the schoolyard!
3. In 44 BC, Julius Caesar was the boss of Rome.
4. Don't eat that! The cat licked it.☒
5. Daddy, why is the grass green? Why is the sky blue? ☒
6. If you mix blue and red together, you get purple. ☒
7. P. T. Barnum was a great circus owner in the late 1800s. ☒
8. Rats! I just stepped in mud with my brand new shoes!
9. Is the male peacock prettier than the female? ☒

## Apostrophes
### Apostrophes 1 (p. 48)

| | | |
|---|---|---|
| Aaron's | Isla's | Tiger's |
| Olive's | Roz's | Carlos's |
| Maya's | Thomas's | Judi's |
| Cass's | Jade's | Charles's |
| Ashley's | Alexis's | Brittany's |

### Apostrophes 2 (p. 49)

BOYS' LOCKERS

WOMEN'S ROOM

LADIES' CHANGING AREA

GIRLS' LOCKERS

INSTRUCTORS' LOUNGE

PEOPLE'S GARDEN

EMPLOYEES' ENTRANCE

MEN'S ROOM

MICE'S CHEESE STORAGE AREA

CHILDREN'S PLAYGROUND

### Apostrophes 3 (p. 50)

sister-in-law's silver shoes in the red suitcase

great-grandmother's lace shawl in the large trunk

six-year-old's favorite books in the small trunk

brothers-in-law's socks in the blue backpack

son-in-law's gym shorts in the green duffel bag

mother-in-law's wallet in the leather handbag

great-aunt's glasses in the over-the-shoulder bag

great-grandfather's suspenders in the valise

father-in-law's coonskin cap in the hat box

step-sister's fancy gown in the garment bag

### Apostrophes 4 (p. 51)

Arlene's and Jack's phones

Ellen, Anne, and Consuela's umbrella

Glenn and Laurie's sofa

Rajeev, Neena, and Sharmila's carriage

### Apostrophes 5 (p. 52)

1. She doesn't know if we've got enough money or if we haven't. **3**
2. Shouldn't you be asking if we'll arrive on time or if we'd be wise to turn back before it's too late? **4**
3. I'm sorry, but she'll have to wait her turn or they'll all get angry before you've sung the song. **4**
4. My sister can't run that fast, so you'll just have to slow down or she'll make us go home earlier than we'd expected. **4**
5. They're the ones he's been talking about because they wouldn't give him any cookies. **3**

6. They'll love the new teacher because he's very nice and that'll make them happy. **3**

7. I've walked six miles to see them, but they're not home, and they should've been, so that's all I have to say about that. **4**

8. Aren't you worried that there's going to be a snowstorm tonight and we won't be able to go to school tomorrow? **3**

9. If he hadn't said what he said, she wouldn't have said what she said, and they would've had a better time at the party, don't you think? **4**

10. What's that, and where's the thingamajig, and who's he, and when's the show, and who'd like to go? **5**

Answer: 37

A starfish has 5 arms, so 7 starfish have 35 arms. A monkey has 2 arms. 35 + 2 = 37.

### Apostrophes 6 (p. 53)

Math Students: Don't confuse your 6s and your 9s.

Test Takers: Put ✓'s in the boxes next to the correct answers.

Game Players: To play Tic-Tac-Toe, first draw a lot of #'s.

Handwriters: Carefully dot your i's and cross your t's.

High School Juniors: Get DVDs to help you study for your SATs.

Spellers: Spell "Mississippi" with four i's and "muumuu" with four u's.

E-mailers: Put @'s into e-mail addresses.

Everybody: "Mind your p's and q's." (Behave yourselves.)

### Apostrophes Tic-Tac-Toe (p. 54)

1. The children's room is very messy.

2. I've always thought that it isn't nice to say, "Wow, that was loud!" when someone sneezes.

3. In the 1800s women wore big dresses. ☒

4. The men's room is on the fourth floor; the women's room is down the hall.

5. My school's music room is decorated from floor to ceiling with ♪'s. ☒

6. Her brother-in-law's dog is smaller than my sister-in-law's cat.

7. Are there any ATMs around here? ☒

8. Abdulkareem and Wildan's house is in Iraq. ☒

9. The banker's tie is decorated with hundreds of $'s. ☒

## Quotation Marks

### Quotation Marks 1 (p. 56)

I got the call at 10:15 a.m., Saturday morning. "My science project is missing!" shouted a boy named David.

"I'll be right over," I said, and off I went. I asked David, "Can you describe it to me?"

"It's made up of a lot of fun stuff like wheels, and gears, and switches, and it lights up and rings bells," he said.

"When did you see it last?" I inquired.

The boy said, "Last night. Jennifer, my kid sister, was playing with it."

So I asked Jennifer, "Do you know where it is?"

Laughing, she pointed under her bed. "There!" she shouted.

David's sister liked playing with it so much, she didn't want him to take it to school.

"Thanks for finding it," said David's mother.

His father added, "David worked on it for a month."

"I'm glad I could help," I answered.

"I'll be more careful next time," David said.

His little sister gurgled, "Bye, bye."

As I left, I thought to myself, "Boy, I'm good," and I am!

### Quotation Marks 2 (p. 57)

When I first met Ms. Missouri, I asked her, "Who are your best friends in show business?" and she thought for a moment.

Finally, she answered, "I've known Jane Maine and Alexis Texas for a long time," but before she could say anything else, there was a knock on the dressing room door. Lorrie open it, exclaimed, "I can't believe it!" and started jumping up and down with joy.

I recognized the two young women entering the dressing room and inquired, "Della Delaware and Candice Kansas, what are you doing here?" but they ignored me and rushed to their friend Lorrie.

Lorrie stopped jumping for a moment and said, "They are here to see me star in my new show, of course," and then she hugged her friends.

Della and Candice burst into big grins and announced together, "We have a surprise for you," and right behind them I saw none other than Virginia Virginia and Georgia Georgia.

By now the dressing room was getting crowded with teen stars, so Lorrie suggested, "Let's go outside for some fresh air," and they all ran out, leaving me behind.

And that, folks, is my exclusive interview with Lorrie Missouri. You won't read it in any other magazine.

### Quotation Marks 3 (p. 58)

1. "To be or not to be," said Hamlet, "that is the question."

2. "Think of all the beauty still left around you," Anne Frank wrote in her diary, "and be happy."

3. "History will be kind to me," remarked Winston Churchill, "for I intend to write it."

4. "I have failed many times," Michael Jordan admitted, "and that's why I am a success."

5. "If you tell the truth," advised Mark Twain, "you don't have to remember anything."

6. "A slip of the foot you may soon recover," wrote Benjamin Franklin, "but a slip of the tongue you may never get over."

7. "Keep your face to the sunshine," Helen Keller recommended, "and you cannot see the shadow."

8. "We must learn to live together as brothers," said Martin Luther King, Jr., "or perish together as fools."

9. "It is not fair to ask of others," wrote Eleanor Roosevelt, "what you are unwilling to do yourself."

10. "I never ran my train off the track," Harriet Tubman declared, "and I never lost a passenger."

### Quotation Marks 4 (p. 59)

Music: Learn the song "A Night to Remember" from *High School Musical 3* to sing at the talent show.

Art History: Find out why Leonardo da Vinci's painting "Mona Lisa" is also called "La Gioconda."

Literature: Read the chapter called "Castle in the Air" from *The Phantom Tollbooth*.

Science: Watch the episode called "Your Nose" on *The Amazing Human Body* tonight at 8:00 p.m. on Channel 66, and be sure to take notes.

Journalism: Interview a teacher and write an article for the school newspaper called "My Teacher's Favorite Things."

Art: Find pictures online of the famous statue "The Thinker" by Auguste Rodin and think about it.

Playwriting: Write a short play called "Nobody Will Believe This" that begins with the sentence, "Nobody will believe this."

Poetry: Underline all the words you don't know in the poem "When Cats Bark" from the book *Animal Poetry*.

Public Speaking: Watch the video of a speech Barack Obama gave called "The American Promise" and find out what the promise is.

### Quotation Marks 5 (p. 60)

1. Wilt "the Stilt" Chamberlain, the great basketball player, was over 7 feet tall.

2. Because a $100 bill has Ben Franklin's picture on it, some people call it a "Benjamin."

3. After he failed all his exams, his friends started calling him "The Brain," but he didn't like the joke.

4. She rented a "furnished" apartment over the phone, but it had only a window shade and shower curtain.

5. President Eisenhower was called "Ike," and President Lincoln was known as "Honest Abe."

6. The so-called "food" they serve in the cafeteria tastes like cardboard and rubber.

7. My brother wouldn't go to that movie with us because he thought it was a "chick flick."

8. The "free" sample I ordered cost over $10 for shipping and handling!

9. The new student from England says we're his "mates," calls gym shoes "plimsolls," and goes on "holiday" when we take our vacation.

10. That "easy" test the teacher promised had 100 questions!

### Quotation Marks 6 (p. 61)

QUIZMASTER: Contestant #1, your first word is arglebargle.

CONTESTANT 1: Oh, that's easy. Arglebargle means "an argument."

CONTESTANT 2: No, it doesn't.

CONTESTANT 1: Yes, it does!

QUIZMASTER: Let's not have an arglebargle about it.

CONTESTANT #2: This show is giving me collywobbles.

QUIZMASTER: What are those?

CONTESTANT #1: *Collywobbles* means "stomach pains."

CONTESTANT #2: That's because you're trying to bamboozle me, and *bamboozle* means "to cheat somebody."

CONTESTANT #1: I won't stand for this jiggery-pokery any more.

QUIZMASTER: *Jiggery-pokery* means "dishonest behavior," folks.

CONTESTANT #2: I'm totally flabbergasted!

QUIZMASTER: That means "astonished." And so am I. I've got to end this kerfuffle (a "commotion or ruckus") immediately.

CONTESTANT #1: This is worse than a kerfuffle. It's a brouhaha!

CONTESTANT #2: I know that word. *Brouhaha* means "a kerfuffle."

QUIZMASTER: I've had enough of this arglebargle, jiggery-pokery, kerfuffle, and brouhaha. I'm getting collywobbles, too. I'm going home.

### Quotation Marks Tic-Tac-Toe (p. 62)

1. "Don't forget to walk the goat after dinner," said his mother. ☒

   He shouted, "This is the greatest thing that ever happened to me!" ☒

2. "I would if I could," she yelled, "but I can't, so I won't." ☒

3. I never knew that hullabaloo means "a hubbub," which means "an excited fuss." Did you?

4. Someone ripped out an article from this magazine entitled "Don't Rip Out This Article." ☒

5. "I thought I lost my cell phone," said my father, "but it was right on the table where I left it."

6. I liked all the poems in this book except the one called "The Mouse in the House."

7. My British cousin calls the elevator a "lift." ☒

8. Because he has a lot of allergies, we call my brother "Sneezy."

## Colons & Semicolons

### Colons & Semicolons 1 (p. 64)

To: All Employees
From: The New Boss
Subject: About Me
Date: Today

Many of you have asked me to tell you about myself, so here goes:

I have five dogs: Winston, Woodrow, Wilson, Waylon, and Sam.

I enjoy the following activities after work: going home and taking a nap.

My favorite foods all begin with *k*: kumquats, kiwi, knishes, and kale—all covered in ketchup.

I have a great theory about eating: Start with dessert because you might be too full for it at the end of the meal.

Here are the names you can call me: Mr. Muffin, Sam, or Boss.

The best lesson I ever learned in my life was this: Don't try to whistle while eating crackers and peanut butter.

After just one day on this job, I have come to this conclusion: I like it here!

## Colons & Semicolons 2 (p. 65)

Dear Clean Air Committee:

Vegetarians:

To Whom It May Concern:

To All Pet Owners:

Dear Vegetable Association:

All Clowns:

To the Office of Proper Dress:

Dear Repair Department:

## Colons & Semicolons 3 (p. 66)

Detective: At what time did all the lights go out?

Witness 1: 6:23 a.m.

Witness 2: No, it was 7:13 a.m.

Witness 3: I disagree. It was more like 8:33 a.m.

Detective: Well, what time did they go back on?

Witness 1: Sometime between 9:53 a.m. and 10:43 a.m.

Witness 2: No, no. It was much closer to 8:40 a.m.

Witness 3: I disagree again. It was much later. Probably around 11:50 a.m.

Detective: Well, what time was lunch served?

Witness 1: The same time it always is: 12:30 p.m.

Witness 3: I disagree again. I didn't get my lunch until 1:15. I was starving!

Detective: Well, that solves the case.

Witnesses 1, 2, and 3: What case?

Detective: The case of when the lights went out!

Witnesses 1, 2, and 3: Well, when did they go out?

Detective: At exactly 7:47 a.m.

Witnesses 1, 2, and 3: How did you discover that?

Detective: It was on the news. There was a blackout at that moment all over the city.

Witnesses 1, 2, and 3: You're brilliant!

Detective: I know. And modest, too. Oh, it's 4:26 p.m. I have to get back to the station.

## Colons & Semicolons 4 (p. 67)

1. Her uncle is the butcher; her aunt makes the hamburgers.

2. It rains a lot here in April; it's great for growing flowers.

3. Grandpa looks great with his beard; he should have grown it years ago.

4. It's been raining for three days; it's great weather for ducks.

5. She's been studying astronomy; she loves the stars.

6. Everest is the highest mountain on Earth; Cotahuasi, in Peru, is the deepest canyon.

7. A hamburger has no ham in it; a hot dog is not a dog.

## Colons & Semicolons 5 (p. 68)

Little Red Riding Hood to the Big Bad Wolf: You ate my grandmother; as a result, I'm not your friend.

Big Bad Wolf to Little Red Riding Hood: People think I'm mean; on the contrary, I'm a nice guy. Really.

Goldilocks to The Three Bears: I slept in your beds; in addition, I ate your porridge. Sorry.

Snow White to the Seven Dwarfs: I'm a great housekeeper; for example, I can clean, cook, and sew.

Big Bad Wolf to the Three Little Pigs: I'll huff and I'll puff; in fact, I'll blow your houses down.

Little Miss Muffet to the Spider: You frightened me away; nevertheless, I'm coming back for my curds and whey.

Prince Charming to Cinderella: Your foot fit the glass slipper; for this reason, I'll marry you.

Beauty to the Beast: You are a beast; on the other hand, beasts can be lovable, too.

Hansel to Gretel: It's getting dark; moreover, we're lost in the woods. Yikes!

Jill to Jack: Let's go up the hill again; however, don't fall down this time.

## Colons & Semicolons 6 (p. 69)

You'll love . . .

Paula Paws, the animal trainer, and her dancing bear, Twinkletoes; Mr. Stretch, the world's tallest man, and his little dog, Pooch; and Blaze and Flame, the fire-eating frogs.

You'll cheer for . . .

Swing and Sway, the daredevil trapeze artists; Boom, the human cannonball; and Chewy, the fearless man who sticks his head in a lion's mouth.

You'll laugh at . . .

Mr. Fingers, who juggles bubbles, feathers, and water; Frosting and Crumbs, the pie-throwing dogs; and Henny, the singing chicken.

## Colons & Semicolons Tic-Tac-Toe (p. 70)

1. Father: How did you do on your report card?
Son: Like Abraham Lincoln.
Father: What do you mean?
Son: I went down in history.

2. Take these items to the yard sale: your old CDs, your dad's typewriter, and the green hula hoops. ☒

3. To: The Sales Dept.
From: Customer Service
Date: Aug. 14, 2010
Subject: The New Can Opener
It doesn't work!

4. The chicken played the piano; the rabbit danced.

5. The day was beautiful: sunny, warm, and breezy. ☒

6. Ticket Holders: Line up single file. Don't push!

7. To the members of Congress: Hello there.
Jimmy ☒

8. If you leave at 7:45 a.m., and there's no traffic, you'll get to school by 8:10 a.m., at the latest. ☒

9. The dam burst and flooded the town; consequently, the parade was canceled. ☒